ARTIFICIAL INTELLIGENCE AND THE BUREAUCRATIC BLACK BOX IN CAREER AND TECHNICAL EDUCATION

By

Dr. Jacinda H. Lay, EdD

ARTIFICIAL INTELLIGENCE AND THE BUREAUCRATIC BLACK BOX IN CAREER AND TECHNICAL EDUCATION

Dr. Jacinda H. Lay, EdD

Dedication

To every educator, every change agent, and every innovator out there who shows up ready to break down the walls of bureaucracy, making education equitable for everyone.

To my students, you are the reason for all of this. Your resilience, your grit, and your sheer determination inspire me every single day.

Acknowledgment

This book exists because of the support of many individuals who saw the necessity of this work and helped me bring it to light.

The Change Agents and Intellectual Guides

I first want to thank the many fellow educators and innovators across the Career and Technical Education (CTE) landscape who risk comfort to pursue truth. Your stories, your frustrated committee meetings, and your quiet victories against inertia were the essential fuel for this analysis.

I am profoundly grateful to Sharon Bonney, the Chief Executive Officer at the Coalition on Adult Basic Education. Thank you, Sharon, for the front-row seat as a State Advocate for Adult Education Fellow and for giving me your time and guidance when I cannot seem to find my way through the professional and political terrains that come with adult education.

Personal and Emotional Foundation

Finally, to those who provided the unwavering home base, the support that allowed me to enter the Black Box and emerge intact:

To my partner, Jess St. Peter, thank you for the quiet hours, and the indispensable belief that this story needed to be told. You are the ultimate source of my transparency.

To my sister Nidia Parsons for reminding me how strong we really are as women, giving up is not an option.

To our mother who has passed, yet I still feel her near me every day listening to my voice when no one else will.

Lastly, to my father for teaching me there is never too much determination if you believe.

Dr. Jacinda H. Lay, EdD

Authors Note on the use of Artificial Intelligence

In the research and drafting of this book, the author made limited use of large language model based artificial intelligence tools, including OpenAI's ChatGPT and Google's Gemini. These tools were used as writing and thinking aids, for example to clarify language, explore alternative phrasings, summarize publicly available material, and support structural revision.

All arguments, interpretations, conclusions, and critical judgments presented in this book are the author's own. Artificial intelligence tools did not determine the analytical framework, select sources, or make evaluative decisions.

The use of these systems is disclosed intentionally. This book argues that opaque systems erode trust and accountability in education and governance. Transparency in authorship and method is therefore not incidental to the argument. It is part of it.

Contents

Epigraph

The true significance of bureaucracy is precisely that it develops the more perfectly the more it is 'dehumanized,' the more completely it succeeds in eliminating from official business love, hatred, and purely personal, irrational, and emotional elements which escape calculation.

— **Max Weber**

Key Terms and Definitions

The Change Agent

The label "change agent" itself is political. A change agent is a person, group, or organization that helps a system improve by enhancing its processes, structures, or everyday practices (Ungvarsky, 2025). Change agents understand the context and the people involved. They recognize what needs to change and are motivated to design new ways of doing things. Change agents are uniquely disruptive for bureaucratic systems. They work within organizations but often question unwritten rules. Effective change agents tend to have strong inner qualities such as creativity, courage, persistence, and a sense of moral purpose. They also possess practical skills to plan and implement change in real-world conditions (Gerwing, 2016; Wireman, 1998).

What Is Artificial Intelligence (AI)?

In this book, Artificial Intelligence in education means the use of computer systems and algorithms that learn from data to detect patterns and make predictions. Artificial Intelligence is the ability of machines to mimic some human thinking in tasks such as decision making, speech recognition, pattern detection, and even serving as a thought partner. It includes methods such as machine learning and deep learning, where algorithms are trained on data to recognize patterns and improve their decisions over time (Saini et al., 2025).

As AI capabilities grow, they affect many areas, including speech recognition, customer service, and content generation, and they raise ongoing questions about ethics, transparency, and responsible use.

Black Box Problem in Artificial Intelligence

Observers can see the inputs and outputs of AI systems but not how they work inside. Because the decision process, especially in deep learning, is opaque, it is hard to know when to trust the results. This black box problem limits trust in AI. Attempts to explain models help but do not fully solve it. Real trust needs transparency in the whole system around AI, including institutions, processes, and oversight. Trust in AI will depend on making that wider system more trustworthy (von Eschenbach, 2021).

The Bureaucratic Black Box

A bureaucratic black box is a decision system where the steps are visible, but the reasoning and power are hidden. On the surface, it follows rules, procedures, and committees. Outsiders cannot see how policies, data, or requests become approvals, denials, budgets, or sanctions. Explanations such as "that is the policy" or "the decision has been made" hide interests, risk avoidance, and politics. This protects institutional authority, makes decisions look rule based, and obscures who is responsible, which values guided the choice, and how it could be questioned or changed.

Disclaimer

This book is designed to provide information and analysis regarding bureaucracy education, and Artificial Intelligence. The information is presented based on the author's research and experience. While the author has made every effort to ensure the accuracy of the information within this book, the information shared is for educational and critical analysis purposes only. The author and publisher shall not have any liability or responsibility to any person or entity with respect to any loss or damage caused or alleged to be caused directly or indirectly by the information contained in this book.

PROLOGUE

The mythological figure most linked to a box is Pandora. She was given a container and told not to open it. She opened it anyway and released sickness, death, and other harms into the world. Only hope stayed inside. "Pandora's box" now means an action that seems small but leads to trouble.

For more than twenty years as a Change Agent in Career and Technical Education, that has been my metaphor. Today, Career and Technical Education faces its own box. We are putting Artificial Intelligence into systems shaped by bureaucracy. This is the Bureaucratic Black Box, a set of policies, procedures, and power relationships that can keep order but also block change.

This book is about that risk. A rush to use AI to make educational systems more efficient can also increase complexity, hide decisions, and deepen inequities. The problem is not only the technology, but how it is used in an organization built to protect itself. I have seen structures that maintain predictability, reward compliance, and resist changes that threaten the hierarchy. I have seen new tools, teaching methods, and policies pushed aside while Change Agents are praised in words and limited in practice.

AI sharpens this conflict. It can support learning, improve curriculum, and make processes more open. It can also be turned into another tool of control. AI measures work rather than popularity, pushes toward clearer data, and spreads knowledge beyond central offices. Bureaucracy often reacts against that.

This book looks at that clash in Career and Technical Education. It describes how bureaucracy works in CTE, how it shapes decisions, and why it is hard to change. It also considers how AI could support a model of education that is more open, fair, and effective, and what happens when AI is used instead to protect existing power.

The Black Box here is not only a way to describe hidden technology. It also represents systems of control that slow change in education. This is the story of a new tool for transparency meeting an old structure of resistance. I wrote this book because I believe the future of technical education and merit based opportunity depends on how this conflict is resolved. The risk is that the Bureaucratic Black Box will not only release harm, but also weaken the hope needed to keep innovation alive in systems that still favor conformity over progress.

Introduction: The Black Box

Every few years, a major innovation arrives promising to solve the systemic challenges of public education. I have watched many such waves roll through: collaborative learning mandates, new accountability frameworks, standardized testing regimes, and, most recently, Artificial Intelligence (AI). After years of working in Career and Technical Education (CTE), I have observed as a change agent how visionary leaders attempt reforms that promise to elevate instructors, improve student outcomes, and modernize outdated systems. Yet almost every attempt runs into the same barrier: bureaucracy. Administrators who hold power either consciously or unconsciously sustain an industrial-era structure whose true purpose is to maintain authority and prevent any change that might disrupt the dynamics of institutional power.

The black box problem in AI is fundamentally similar to the bureaucratic black box because both hide how decisions are actually made while still producing authoritative outcomes. In AI, especially deep learning systems, observers can see the data going in and the decisions coming out, but the internal decision process remains opaque. Similarly, in bureaucracy, people see forms submitted, committees convened, and final approvals or denials, but the real reasons, trade-offs, and informal politics that shape those decisions remain hidden. In both cases, the crucial path from input to decision is obscured from those most affected by it.

Both systems also protect themselves through claims of neutrality. AI decisions are framed as objective outputs of "the algorithm," while bureaucratic decisions are framed as merely following "policy and procedure." This rhetoric shifts accountability away from individual decision makers and onto "the system," making it harder to question or contest outcomes. Those outside the system lack knowledge of information needed to understand, challenge and decisions made.

When AI is embedded inside a bureaucracy, these black boxes stack on top of each other. An opaque AI model operates within an already opaque institutional structure. Leaders can then say, "the data and the system require this," while concealing both the algorithmic logic and the bureaucratic choices about what data to use, which metrics to prioritize, and who gets access. This is what I refer to as Bureaucratic AI: artificial intelligence reshaped to reinforce bureaucratic control rather than increase transparency, making power harder to see and even harder to challenge.

PART I

The Bureaucratic Machine

Chapter 1

Century Old Architecture

Behind Blind Bureaucracy

Resistance to Artificial Intelligence (AI) in education is often described as a fear of new technology, but this narrative is historically inaccurate. Today's administrative leaders are not reacting to AI; they are fulfilling an organizational design established more than a century ago. To understand why educational institutions instinctively avoid transparency, resist neutralism, and cling to centralized control, we must examine both the origins of American school bureaucracy and how these structures continue to suffocate innovation.

Bureaucracy emerged from this historical context as a structural necessity, a protective enclosure for administrative authority. Routines, procedures, and reporting systems became mechanisms through which the managerial class preserved its power and maintained stability. The goal was not educational excellence but bureaucratic predictability. Compliance outweighed creativity, and conformity was treated as a civic virtue. Innovations that threaten hierarchy, especially those that generate transparency, are perceived as existential threats. The Black Box, born from industrial design, now functions as the invisible center of decision-making. It is a system built to absorb or neutralize any idea that introduces uncertainty, decentralizes authority, or elevates expertise outside of administrative control.

The concept of bureaucracy is fundamentally associated with the German sociologist Max Weber, who developed a rational legal model characterized by hierarchical structure, division of labor, standard operations in continuity of practice. Weber predicted that bureaucracy would be an enduring and difficult-to-destroy social structure, largely confirmed by its adaptability across public and private organizations, including educational systems (Humes, 2021).

While Weber's model has proven persistent, it has also been amplified by critics who focus on its destructive potential with organizational form and human capacity (Humes, 2021). Weber viewed bureaucracy as an efficient way to make decisions, but he and later critics also highlighted its drawbacks: excessive demand to follow rules, loss of individual freedom, self-serving elites, monotony, alienation, and depersonalization (Humes, 2021). Ehrich and English (2024) argue that educational systems clearly reflect these bureaucratic features. They exhibit hierarchical structures, defined roles, and extensive rules that shape the daily experiences of teachers, students, and administrators. Power in these systems is complex, contested, and fluid. Educational leaders must engage critically with bureaucracy if they hope to achieve meaningful transformation, especially during major reforms.

Since the 1990s, post-bureaucratic organizations has emerged, emphasizing dialogue, consensus, networks, and devolved responsibility over formal authority. This discourse uses terms like partnership, collaboration, empowerment, and collegiality, and it is evident in modern leadership concepts such as distributed leadership. Lumby (2019) contends that claims about distributed leadership, particularly regarding the redistribution of power, are questionable; those in formal authority still retain control over the bureaucratic levers of decision-making (Humes, 2021). Bureaucracy also defends itself through strategic ambiguity. Many policies are crafted or maintained with just enough vagueness to allow administrators broad interpretive authority. This ambiguity enables inconsistent enforcement, shields leaders from accountability, and allows political considerations, rather than student benefit, to drive decision-making.

Ambiguity keeps power centralized and ensures that reforms dependent on clarity, especially those rooted in data-driven insights, can be dismissed or delayed without ever being explicitly rejected. As Ehrich and English (2024) observe, ambiguity is always treated as the villain, and any variation becomes a target for identification and elimination. Ultimately, bureaucratic institutions must be understood in context. Their legitimacy, powers, and resources are tied to political decisions and specific historical and cultural roots. These historical foundations continue to structure how modern bureaucracy resists visionary leadership.

When Artificial Intelligence (AI) enters this environment, it does not simply introduce a new tool it disrupts the century old architecture that bureaucracy was designed to protect. AI systems measure competence rather than compliance. By generating transparency, AI destabilizes a system built on ambiguity. The technology threatens central control through decentralized knowledge and challenges bureaucratic secrecy by exposing inefficiencies. AI is not resisted because it is new; it is resisted because it undermines the fundamental logic of the Black Box. The conflict is not technological but structural, a nineteenth-century managerial design colliding with twenty-first-century tools engineered for merit-based transparency.

Chapter 2

Social Anatomy of the Bureaucratic Black Box

This chapter reveals a deeper, more enduring truth: bureaucratic power is not rooted in policy but in people. It is not the written rules that determine whether an institution embraces or rejects change, it is the unwritten rules that ultimately decide which ideas survive and which are extinguished before they can take root. The Bureaucratic Black Box is not a machine it is a social ecosystem maintained by individuals who instinctively protect their shared interests and reinforce their collective legitimacy.

To understand why Artificial Intelligence (AI) fails in career and technical education, one must first understand this human system. No innovation can succeed in an environment where social power outweighs merit. Every educational institution presents itself as a hierarchy governed by job titles, reporting structures, and written expectations. Yet, anyone embedded in career and technical education quickly learns that the formal hierarchy is a façade. The real hierarchy operates behind the scenes, where authority is conferred not by position but by acceptance into the informal administrative circle.

Within this structure, belonging carries more weight than competence. Once an individual is embraced by the inner circle, their ideas are assumed to be strategic, appropriate, and aligned with institutional goals, regardless of quality. Conversely, those outside the circle often find their expertise dismissed as merely operational or anecdotal.

The inner circle retains its power through patronage and mutual understanding. Members shield one another from scrutiny and present a united front in public, even when internal decisions lack pedagogical or operational merit. This protective layer ensures that administrative mistakes, inefficiencies, and contradictions remain hidden beneath polished narratives of innovation and excellence. The social mechanics of loyalty and protection matter more than policy or organizational structure that institutions claim to follow.

Information control is the most powerful instrument within this bureaucratic social order. The Bureaucratic Black Box is not a technical barrier but a strategy for maintaining dominance. The less information others possess, the more valuable the gatekeepers become. Administrators regulate access to budget details, data reports, and resource allocations to centralize interpretive authority. By controlling who knows what and when, they define the narrative that drives the social order who claim success.

Institutions rely heavily on symbolic capital, titles, committees, awards, and leadership designations to determine whose voice carries weight. Symbolic capital often overshadows genuine expertise, creating a hierarchy where administrative opinions supersede the knowledge of instructors who work directly with students. Symbolic authority is easier to defend than performance-based authority. Once symbolic legitimacy becomes the currency of influence, subject-matter experts struggle to gain traction, even when their insights are grounded in authentic student needs and industry expectations.

Ultimately, the real seat of bureaucratic power resides not in policies or procedures, nor in organizational structures or job descriptions, but in the social contract that binds the social circle together. This contract is built on an implicit agreement to protect one another, preserve the hierarchy, maintain institutional narratives, and prevent transparency that could lead to accountability. Until this contract is confronted directly, innovations will continue to fail. No technological tool can succeed in an environment where social power determines institutional decisions.

Chapter 3

The Change Agent Stands

Where?

A change agent is a person, group, or organization that helps a system improve by enhancing its processes, structures, or everyday practices (Ungvarsky, 2025). Change agents can come from inside or outside an organization, but they share core abilities. They understand the context and the people involved. Change agents recognize what needs to change and are motivated to design new ways of doing things. Change agents explain why the change is necessary and how it will happen (Ungvarsky, 2025). Often, they act as researchers, planners, and mentors, using strong relationships, organizational skills, and communication to help others overcome resistance and ensure that change lasts (Ungvarsky, 2025).

In schools, teachers can be especially powerful change agents. They are not transmitters of knowledge; they can question existing practices, build new approaches, and respond to the needs of students and communities. In times of conflict, teachers help build resilience, raise awareness, and strengthen social preparedness, acting as agents of change at individual, institutional, and societal levels (Gokmenoglu et al., 2025).

Research also shows that true change agents are uniquely disruptive for bureaucratic systems. They work within organizations but often questions unwritten rules. Many change efforts fail, even when the pressure to adapt is obvious, because leaders underestimate how much success depends on the people who design, carry out, and interpret change in everyday practice (Gerwing, 2016). Effective change agents tend to have strong inner qualities such as creativity, courage, persistence, and a sense of moral purpose. They also possess practical skills to plan and implement change in real-world, conditions (Gerwing, 2016; Wireman, 1998). In schools, teacher change agents are most effective when they combine these traits with strong positions in social networks, the ability to build trust, and the skill to present new practices as both appealing and realistic (Brown et al., 2021).

Because change agents surface uncomfortable truths and question routine ways of working, their success can expose the limits of those in power. As a result, they are more likely to be sidelined, not because their ideas lack value, but because their ideas reveal how fragile bureaucratic authority can be. The label "change agent" itself is political. Many organizations still select change agents through subjective, relationship-based decisions, which employees see as biased and political (Mashhady et al., 2022). To counter this, Mashhady and colleagues propose a transparent, competency-based group decision system that evaluates candidates on character, leadership, social and political skills, and strategic and technical skills through a participatory process.

Unless organizations adopt fair, competency-based selection methods that truly value those who challenge the status quo, most official "change agents" will end up protecting the bureaucracy rather than pushing for change (Gerwing, 2016; Mashhady et al., 2022; Wireman, 1998; Brown et al., 2021; Ungvarsky, 2025). When AI begins to reveal bias, inefficiency, or incompetence, genuine change agents become translators of those uncomfortable findings, inviting scrutiny of long- protected people and processes. Without intentional support and protection for these individuals, even well-designed reforms and AI's potential to support them are likely to be tamed into tools that manage appearances instead of transforming practice.

PART II

Career and Technical College Context

Chapter 4

Industrial Blueprint

AI Reshapes Career and Technical Education

Education, as a political and sociocultural practice, has continually evolved alongside major technological revolutions, including shifts in career and technical education (CTE) (Dai et al., 2025). In the first industrial revolution, steam power shifted societies from farming to manufacturing. Education, including early forms of vocational and craft training, mainly served agrarian and craft-based economies for the elite and was controlled by local authorities with strong hierarchy and standardization.

The second industrial revolution, driven by electricity and mass production, brought ideas of efficiency. Education expanded and became more standardized, with growing emphasis on preparing a skilled and specialized workforce through formal schooling and emerging technical and vocational programs. The third industrial revolution introduced digitalization and automation. Computers, the internet, and digital platforms entered schools, enabling data-driven decisions and supporting more flexible, student-centered models. CTE began to incorporate digital tools, technical training, and industry-aligned skills, although technology was still largely seen as a separate tool to improve efficiency.

Today can be considered the fourth industrial revolution integrates AI, robotics, big data, cloud computing, and the Internet of Things, blurring the boundaries between physical, digital, and biological worlds. AI supports tasks such as tutoring, assessment, and technical skills training, and educational leaders, especially in CTE, must develop strong data literacy to manage complex, real-time information (Dai et al., 2025).

Artificial Intelligence in education refers to the use of computer systems that learn from data to spot patterns and make predictions. Artificial Intelligence (AI) is the ability of computers and machines to mimic human intelligence and carry out tasks such as decision-making, speech recognition, pattern detection, and even acting as a thought partner. It includes technologies like machine learning and deep learning, in which algorithms are trained on data to recognize patterns, emulate aspects of human decision processes, and improve their predictions over time (Saini et al., 2025). As AI capabilities continue to expand, they are increasingly influencing a wide range of areas, including speech recognition, customer service, and content generation, while also raising important conversations around ethics, transparency, and responsible use.

In the context of Artificial Intelligence (AI), several terms define specific technologies and methodologies. Machine Learning (ML) is an AI discipline that employs mathematical and statistical techniques to identify patterns and regularities within data sets. This process enables a system to independently construct models, make predictions, and take actions based on these predictive models as it accumulates knowledge through experience (Botev et al., 2025).

Deep Learning (DL) is a subset of ML (Nkadimeng et al.,2024) that leverages neural networks with multiple layers and backpropagation algorithms to perform complex tasks. These tasks include image categorization, natural language processing, and identifying patterns within extensive data sets (Deshpande & Sharma, 2025). There are AI models designed to comprehend context and the relationships between words in a sentence. This enhances their capability to generate clear and coherent text that is similar to human writing. Generative AI is a broader category that describes systems utilizing large language models, among other design approaches (Ciubotaru, 2025). These systems are trained on vast data volumes and have the capacity to produce new content. This content, which can take the form of text, images, analyses, or music, is generated instead of analyzing or classifying existing data.

Lesson planning with artificial intelligence tools can support teachers in many ways. For example, a teacher might prompt: "Act like a math teacher and create four lesson plans lasting five days each on factoring polynomials. Be sure to provide at least six examples with solutions for students to test their understanding." Artificial intelligence can also help answer student questions by providing quick and accurate explanations when clarification is needed. In creating educational content, AI can assist teachers in generating lesson plans, quizzes, and study guides tailored to their curriculum.

AI can also support the special needs of students by providing accommodations and tailored explanations based on individual requirements. Learning difficulties can seriously affect students' academic performance and overall school experience. Without adequate personalized support, these needs are often overlooked, leading to a downward spiral that limits future educational and career opportunities (Hu, 2024). Special education support can be improved when AI helps professionals create individualized education plans (IEPs) by recommending appropriate interventions and accommodations based on a student's specific needs and abilities. In language learning, AI can be a valuable tool for teachers, engaging students in conversations, helping with pronunciation, and providing practice opportunities (Praveena et al., 2025).

In coding and programming classes, AI can assist students by offering code explanations, debugging tips, and coding examples (Amiri & Islam, 2025). Teachers can also use artificial intelligence to encourage critical thinking by presenting students with challenging questions and prompts that promote creativity and deeper analysis. As a writing assistant, AI can help students improve their writing skills by providing grammar and style suggestions, brainstorming ideas, and assisting with editing and revision. In foreign language learning more broadly, AI chatbots can facilitate practice and immersion in the target language. AI also supports personalized learning by adapting to the needs and progress of individual students. Additionally, educators can use AI for their own professional development, seeking resources, strategies, and explanations to improve their practice.

Operational uses of AI in education extend beyond the classroom and support broader educational functions. In student performance analytics, an educational organization might use AI to analyze standardized test scores, homework completion rates, and attendance records to identify students who may need additional support or enrichment programs. In personalized learning, an AI-driven platform can assess a student's strengths and weaknesses in mathematics and adjust the difficulty level of math problems in real time to provide a customized learning experience.

Predictive analytics for student interventions can use historical data to identify which students are at risk of not completing their program on time. This allows educators to allocate resources and interventions strategically to help these students stay on track (Cao & Mai, 2025; Herodotou et al., 2020). Chatbots for administrative tasks can be deployed on institutional websites to answer questions about enrollment, policies, and upcoming events, providing instant responses to common inquiries. In terms of security and safety, AI-powered cameras on campuses or in learning environments can detect unusual behavior patterns, such as trespassing or aggressive actions, and immediately alert security personnel.

AI can also support adaptive assessments, such as computer-based evaluations that adjust the difficulty of math questions based on each student's previous answers. This provides tailored feedback and improves learning outcomes (Khine, 2024). For teacher professional development AI can analyze evaluations, student performance data, and educator preferences to suggest relevant learning opportunities, including workshops and online courses.

Engagement with families and stakeholders can be enhanced through AI powered mobile applications that send notifications about homework assignments, test scores, and events, facilitating stronger communication between home and educational institutions. Language translation tools powered by AI can instantly translate announcements and communications into multiple languages, ensuring non-native speakers remain informed.

From an operational and logistical perspective, AI can aid resource allocation by analyzing enrollment projections, learner demographics, and facility utilization data to recommend optimal distribution of educators and classrooms. For curriculum development, AI can analyze textbooks and educational materials, suggesting updates and improvements to align with the latest standards and research.

In human resources and staffing, AI can screen job applicants' résumés and cover letters, highlighting candidates whose qualifications match teaching and support positions, making the hiring process more efficient. Finally, data management and reporting can be streamlined with an AI powered data management system that automatically collects, cleans, and analyzes student performance data, generating comprehensive reports that help educators track progress and make informed decisions.

Sun and Pratt argue that while AI offers clear benefits, it faces significant system level challenges involving culture, funding, and bureaucratic resistance. From this perspective, resistance to AI in career and technical colleges is not merely a fear of technology but also a refusal to adopt tools that would bring accountability, visibility, and precision for administration. The issue is not only technical but political: in institutions built on hierarchy, tradition, and slow procedures, any technology that makes performance more visible and accelerates truth-telling is perceived as a threat.

Looking ahead, the concept of a fifth industrial revolution emphasizes a human-centered, sustainable, and resilient partnership between humans and machines. Post-digital perspectives view technology as embedded in everyday life, shifting attention from innovation itself to its broader social, cultural, and philosophical impacts on schooling and CTE. Under the post-digital condition, the boundary between AI and human decision-making becomes increasingly blurred.

Chapter 5

Specialized AI Threatens Bureaucratic Power

Or is it Just Loss of Control?

Sun and Pratt (2024) show that Career and Technical Education (CTE), because it is hands-on and closely tied to industry, could benefit significantly from AI, even though it is often left out of AI in education discussions. They note that AI can reduce teacher workload, personalize learning, track student progress, and help programs stay aligned with changing industry needs. Yet they also identify major barriers, fear and anxiety, weak policy guidance, limited infrastructure, privacy and ethics concerns, and specific challenges in safety-critical fields. Many CTE teachers and leaders remain in the early stages of learning and experimenting with AI, lacking the time, training, and trusted examples they need (Sun & Pratt, 2024).

There are also serious risks if AI based performance data is used to monitor and control people ranking instructors, justifying cuts, or pushing out struggling students instead of helping them. AI can be attractive to leaders as a seemingly neutral tool for oversight and discipline, but harmful to faculty and staff, who experience it as a loss of control over their work and a threat of being judged by numbers they did not choose and do not trust. Without clear rules and ways to challenge decisions, AI is more likely to worsen inequalities in CTE rather than reduce them.

Welding

My name is Matt and I have taught welding at this technical college for 15 years. In the local union hall, people knew that my students passed certification tests and found work. When the college began using an AI weld vision system that scored each bead on penetration, porosity, and alignment, I liked it. Students could see where their welds were weak and I used the heat maps to coach them.

Midway through the year, leadership introduced a weld quality analytics platform. Program chairs and deans could see average weld scores by section and instructor. No one asked welding instructors how to read the scores or what was acceptable for new students compared to advanced students. I take students with weaker math, language barriers, and no shop experience, so my early scores were lower than those of a colleague who turned some students away. The data did not show any of that instead it was ranked sections.

In my review, the dean showed the data showed my weld scores were below the department average and that I needed an improvement plan. There was no talk about intake, project difficulty, or the way my students usually caught up by the end of the term. The AI system had that growth in its records, but the data showed only midterm scores.

Over the next year, I changed how I taught. I cut back on some projects early in the term and spent more time on the weld patterns that the AI scored higher. I also started telling some students to wait before taking welding. My average score went up and the dean praised me for using the data. I felt less like a welder and more like a test coach. The AI system that had helped students see and improve their welds became a tool for comparing instructors and pushed my teaching toward what fit school standards instead of what fit the levels of comprehensions students should have when entering into a trade.

Practical Nursing

My name is Sarah and I teach in the second semester of a Practical Nursing program at a college that uses a new AI simulation system for medical surgical and long term care. I remember when pass rates and brochures were the main measures of success. Preceptors knew my course as one that sent out safe graduates, even if my class was not easy.

the college started the AI system, I liked it. Each student wears a badge that links their actions in the lab to the platform. It timestamps hand hygiene, checks if they scan wristbands, records dose calculations, and flags missed steps in the five rights of medication safety. It scores clinical choices for pain, wounds, and falls. I can replay a medication pass and show a student where they rushed or skipped a check.

After a few weeks I saw a pattern. In Section A with Olivia, written test scores were high. In simulation, students often missed second identifiers, moved fast through med passes, and created many near miss dosing errors. In my Section B there were more early failures, but the students who stayed did safer med passes, followed sepsis and stroke steps, and had fewer flagged errors. The AI display showed the gap between sections in clear side by side views.

Leadership then moved to control the data. The platform was routed into a central analytic platform that only leadership had access to. Public reports and accreditation documents used only combined numbers, such as overall simulation performance at ninety two percent. Instructor level differences were not visible. In my review, the dean showed me the data and showed that my early pass rate was below the program average and that I should move more simulations into the green zone. There was no talk of which errors were counted or how the low levels were determined.

For instructors and students in the lab, the same data looked different. Raw logs and scenario views were strong teaching tools. I could show where a student missed an ID check, skipped a pain reassessment, or changed over time from first to last run. I used this to explain my strict grading and to show that lower early pass rates linked to stronger final practice.

A struggle followed over what to measure and who could see it. The dean and leadership wanted final scores, not process steps or near misses. They wanted leadership to see the data first and push it back down as key numbers. Good results were defined as fast completion and many green simulations, no matter how students got there.

There is another path. In a few pilot meetings, nursing faculty, preceptors, and students helped design scoring and decide how to use the data. We chose which errors needed extra practice and which should carry stronger weight. Instructors and students saw detailed data first and used it to change labs, ask for smaller groups, or support a case for more simulation hours.

From my view, the risk to leadership is not that AI can see a blood pressure check or a med pass. The risk is that these detailed records show the gap between how the program is described and how safely students work. Whether that leads to more voice for clinical staff or more top down control depends on who controls the platform and who is allowed to speak for what the AI records.

Electrical

My name is Greg and I teach in the second year of the Electrician program at this college. I have been here long enough to see many new initiatives start and end. Many people see me as the instructor who focuses too much on electrical code and moves too slowly. David is the instructor people point to for high enrollment, labs that move fast, and large projects that look good on tours.

When the college added artificial intelligence to lab and job site work, I liked it. Students began using augmented reality hard hats and smart tools tied to one system. Levels and tape measures logged layout, torque wrenches logged tightening values, and testers logged continuity, insulation resistance, and voltage. As students ran circuits, set boxes, strapped conduit, and wired panels, scanners and tablets built a digital copy of each project and checked it against code and the plan. The system marked box fill problems, support spacing problems, misaligned runs, full conduits, wrong labels, and missing protection. Each issue was time stamped and linked to a student, section, and project.

By the end of the first term, the reports did not match the usual story. In Section A with David, the work looked good on visits and in photos. The artificial intelligence data showed about twenty five violations for every one hundred feet of conduit, many box moves and re bends, and many unlabeled or mislabeled circuits. Many inspections passed only after long rework. In my Section B, projects were smaller. The data showed fewer than five violations for every one hundred feet, steady support spacing and box depth, consistent labels, and inspection passes on the first visit in most cases. For the first time, the college could see which work was actually code compliant and ready to use.

As section reports spread, they cut across the measures that leadership liked to use. For years, leaders had pointed to enrollment, completion, employer quotes, and photos of finished work. Now they saw charts with violations per hundred feet, first pass inspection rates, labeling accuracy, and hours of correction. Some small sections were clearly doing cleaner work than sections the college promoted.

Leaders then pulled the artificial intelligence system under their control. Detailed logs and error maps were limited. Instructors saw only summary scores. The data was turned into short claims such as program compliance above ninety four percent. Leadership set new targets for violation rates and rework hours without much input from people who bend conduit and pull wire.

In my review, the dean showed one bar on a screen and spoke about the big picture. Overall compliance and steady enrollment were named as the main goals. I was told that my labs felt slow and that I should speed up projects so students could complete more footage. There was no talk of violations per hundred feet, first pass inspections, or hours that my students did not spend tearing out their own work.

For me and some coworkers, the same data looked very different. The raw logs and project breakdowns were the best teaching tools I had seen. I could show a 3D view of a run and point to the place where strap spacing went out of code or where a box was overfilled. We could replay a failed inspection, then compare the first try to the corrected work. I used the data to defend my approach, showing that smaller projects and a slower pace led to fewer violations, less rework, and better first pass results, and that faster formats raised rework hours.

What followed was a struggle over what would be measured and who would see it. Leaders wanted a few simple indicators and one chart for compliance, rework, and enrollment. They wanted data to move up, be read in meetings, and return as the same kind of evaluations as before. From where I stand with students on the lab floor, the real issue is not the technology. Artificial intelligence does not threaten the trade. It threatens the ability of distant offices to control the story of performance and to slow down accountability. If electricians and apprentices help decide what is measured and how it is read, the system can support safe work and solid code practice. If not, it will be cut down into a few scores that fit old stories and ignore what the system actually sees on each job.

Heating Ventilation and Air Conditioning (HVAC)

My name is Gabe and I teach in the Heating, Ventilation, and Air Conditioning program at this college, and I have been here long enough to see many different teaching fads come and go. On campus I have a particular reputation. Students and colleagues often describe me as too picky and too slow, while my colleague Robert is praised for smooth labs, satisfied students, and jobs that seem to finish quickly. Administrators like to point to his sections when they talk about successful instruction.

When the college built artificial intelligence into every lab job and simulated service call, I actually liked it at first. Students began using smart gauges and cloud connected manifolds that automatically logged pressures, temperatures, superheat and subcool, vacuum levels, and final system performance. The artificial intelligence compared each diagnostic sequence and repair step to manufacturer specifications and standard troubleshooting trees. It recorded whether students checked airflow, verified electrical supply, tested sensors, and confirmed their diagnoses with appropriate measurements before charging or replacing parts. Every action was time stamped and tied to a specific student, instructor, and unit. For someone like me, who believes that proper diagnosis matters more than simply getting cold air out of the vents, this felt like finally having a detailed witness for what really happened on each job.

By the middle of the semester, reports began to contradict the college’s story about section performance. On paper, Robert's section metrics were high. His labs ran smoothly, student feedback was positive, and jobs concluded quickly. However, artificial intelligence reports showed a different pattern. In Robert’s section, students routinely skipped airflow checks, topped off refrigerant instead of performing full recover-and-weigh procedures, and left systems that failed to meet efficiency targets and generated high callback rates in simulations.

In my section, students were more likely to complain that I was too strict, and my satisfaction scores were lower. Yet the data showed that my students pulled proper vacuums, documented leak checks, verified charge by superheat and subcool, and left behind systems that passed performance benchmarks with very little rework. For the first time, the college could see, in precise numbers, which students were actually fixing systems correctly rather than just getting them to limp along for the moment.

As the artificial intelligence platform generated data comparing sections and cohorts, it began to erode the bureaucracy’s preferred indicators. For years, leadership had leaned on enrollment growth, completion rates, student surveys, and a few glowing employer quotes to decide which programs and instructors were high quality. New charts appeared that showed incomplete diagnostic trees, repeat failure rates, unnecessary part replacements, and the percentage of jobs fixed the first time correctly. These numbers did not always favor the highly marketed flagship cohorts. In some cases, a quiet evening section or a small apprenticeship group clearly outperformed the programs that leadership showcased in brochures. The more visible this data became, the harder it was for non-practitioner administrators to maintain control over the narrative of which instructors and formats were strong.

The complete data was only given to a small group of administrators who converted it into simple numbers (e.g., 90%+ AI accuracy). Leadership then set goals based on these aggregate reports, imposing targets without ever consulting instructors who understood the specific metrics crucial for safety and system longevity.

In my annual review, the dean pulled up the new data, which pointed to a set of summary bars, and said, "We are focused on raising these overall scores across the program. Your responsibility is to move your section closer to the program average on completion time and student satisfaction while keeping these green indicators high." There was no discussion of unnecessary part replacements, missed airflow checks, or the difference between a system that feels cold and a system that is properly charged and tested.

For those of us who work directly with students in the lab, the same data felt very different. The live artificial intelligence logs were the best teaching tool I had ever had. I could walk a student step by step through their own diagnostic sequence, point to the moment when they skipped an airflow check, show how their vacuum stalled because of a hidden restriction, or compare their first and last attempts on the same scenario to highlight real growth. I used the data to defend my supposedly picky approach, demonstrating that my slower labs and stricter expectations produced fewer callbacks and more first-time fixes and that when schedules were compressed or class sizes increased, repeat failures and shortcuts rose sharply.

What followed was a quiet struggle over control. Bureaucracy disliked this HVAC scenario not because it resented technology, but because this kind of artificial intelligence stripped away the ambiguity on which it relied. The system exposed the gap between titles and competence, showing that quieter, lower-status instructors like me sometimes produced far better technicians than highly promoted programs led by instructors like Robert. Real-time analytic platforms shortened decision timelines and demanded concrete responses instead of endless meetings. Detailed logs gave instructors and students evidence they could use to challenge schedule, curriculum, and budget decisions, rather than sending data upward to be interpreted by administrators.

From my vantage point, whether this artificial intelligence becomes a tool for genuine improvement or just another mechanism of control depends entirely on who decides what is measured and how it is read. If HVAC faculty have real authority over that process, the system can support safer, more competent work. If they do not, the bureaucracy will either resist these tools by turning rich diagnostic evidence into simple scores that confirms false data.

Automotive

My name is Gabe and I teach in the Heating, Ventilation, and Air Conditioning program at this college. I have been here long enough to see teaching fads come and go. Students and colleagues often say I am picky and slow. My coworker Robert is praised for labs that move fast, high satisfaction, and jobs that end on time. Administrators point to his sections when they talk about good instruction.

When the college added artificial intelligence to lab jobs and simulated service calls, I liked it. Students used smart gauges and connected manifolds that logged pressures, temperatures, vacuum levels, and system performance. The system checked each job against manufacturer information and basic troubleshooting steps. It recorded whether students checked airflow, power, sensors, and confirmed their diagnosis with measurements before charging or replacing parts. Each action was tied to a student, instructor, and unit.

By the middle of the semester, the reports did not match the usual story about strong sections. On paper, Robert still looked good. His labs stayed on schedule and his students did not complain. The AI logs showed something else. Students in his section often skipped airflow checks, added refrigerant without full recovery and weigh out, and left systems that felt cold but did not meet efficiency goals and showed high callback rates in simulations. In my section, students complained that I was strict and my satisfaction scores were lower. The data showed that my students pulled full vacuums, checked for leaks, set charge by superheat and subcool, and left systems that met performance targets with few returns. For the first time, the college could see which students fixed systems in a solid way instead of just getting them to run for a short time.

As the AI platform compared sections and cohorts, it cut against the indicators that leadership had used. For years, they had focused on enrollment, completion, surveys, and a few employer notes. New charts showed incomplete diagnostic paths, repeat failures, extra parts, and the share of jobs fixed on the first visit. These numbers did not always favor the programs that leadership promoted. In some cases, evening sections or small groups did better than the programs that appeared in brochures.

Leadership then moved to control the HVAC AI system. Detailed logs and job histories that instructors had used in debriefs were replaced with simple scores and summaries. Full data went to leadership, who reduced it to short claims such as overall AI diagnostic accuracy above ninety percent. Leadership set new targets for the share of green jobs and the average score. They did not spend much time asking technicians which measures mattered most for safety and long term performance. In my review, the dean showed the new data and told me to raise completion and satisfaction while keeping the green indicators high. There was no talk of extra parts, missed airflow checks, or the difference between air that feels cold and a system that has been tested and charged in a careful way.

For those of us in the lab, the same data felt useful. The raw AI logs were a strong teaching tool. I could show a student where they skipped an airflow check, where a vacuum stalled, or how their early and later runs on the same problem had changed. I used the data to defend my approach and to show that tight schedules and larger groups led to more repeat failures and more quick shortcuts. Over time, a quiet struggle grew around control. The system showed gaps between titles and skill. It showed that sections with lower status could produce technicians who did better work than promoted programs. It cut the time between weak work and visible results and gave instructors and students records they could use to question schedules, course design, and budgets.

From my point of view, what happens next depends on who controls the measures and how they are read. If HVAC faculty and apprentices share that control, the system can support safer work and better diagnosis. If they do not, central offices will push back or weaken the tools, turning detailed evidence into simple scores that keep the old story about quality in place.

Culinary Arts

My name is Hillary, and I teach in the Culinary Arts program. I focus on the basics, especially knife skills, and some people think my approach is too simple. At the same time, my colleague Chad is always featured in the college's most impressive buffet photos.

When the college brought artificial intelligence into our kitchens, I actually liked it at first. Overhead cameras and sensors started tracking things like knife angle, cut size, portion weight, cooking temperatures, time at each station, and how plates looked. Smart thermometers and scales kept records of key control points, such as the minimum internal temperatures for chicken and seafood, safe holding ranges for hot and cold foods, chill times for sauces, and how much each batch produced. The system checked every plate and prep task against standards for classic cuts, food safety, and portion control. It flagged julienne cuts that were off by more than a couple of millimeters, chicken served below 165 degrees Fahrenheit, steaks that went over 145 degrees, entrées that were more than 15 percent over the portion size, and trays where waste was above the target. Every dish and station got a time stamp and was linked to a specific student, station, and section.

For the first time, we could see not just who made the best-looking plate, but also who kept food safe, portioned correctly, and used ingredients well. By midterm, the data started to show a tough comparison between the two sections. In Section A, which Chad taught, the photos still looked great. Students loved the creative freedom, and his buffets were still the highlight of campus events. But the AI logs told a different story. Only about sixty percent of plates were within the right portion size. Line checks missed the correct hot-holding temperatures about one out of every four times. Waste per cover was twenty-five to thirty percent higher than the program target.

Section A, which Chad led, was even flagged as a high food safety risk because of problems like undercooked chicken and overcooked fish. In my Section B, students sometimes got frustrated with my focus on knife skills. Still, our data was better: over 90 percent of knife cuts were within the right range, 98 percent of plates reached safe temperatures, and waste per cover stayed at or below the target. The numbers showed that my Section B ran more like a professional kitchen, consistently beating Section A on safety, consistency, and cost, even though Chad's section got all the attention.

At that point, I started to feel the bureaucracy closing in. The same AI system that gave me clear teaching data also challenged the college's story about who was the best. Leadership had built Chad up as the top instructor. Now, the numbers showed that his section didn't do as well as my fundamentals class on safety, consistency, and cost. In response, the central office took control of the system. We lost access to detailed cut maps, temperature records, and waste reports. Instructors only got simple scores and color-coded summaries instead of full logs. Most of the data went to research and assessment committees, where it was turned into safe statements like, overall, AI measured plate consistency above 90% and food safety compliance at or above standards.

During my annual review, the dean opened the new dashboard, skipped over the detailed kitchen data, and showed me a page of summary numbers. The dean said, "we are very proud that the program overall is meeting our benchmarks. Your responsibility is to bring your section more in line with our priorities on creativity and student experience, while keeping metrics in an acceptable range." There was no talk about undercooked chicken, overcooked steak, or waste per cover. No one mentioned that my students were hitting knife and food safety targets much more often than the program's star section.

For those of us who work directly with students, the same data meant something else. I could stop a class and show a student exactly where their knife angle changed and their cuts went off. I could pull up a graph of holding temperatures and point out when a pan dropped below a safe range. I could compare two batches and show how better trimming and portioning led to less waste and better results. I started using AI records from class to back up my so-called basic approach, showing that lots of cutting practice and careful attention to temperatures led to safer, more consistent plates with less waste. When we had less time or skipped knife practice, the system quickly showed more mistakes, missed temperatures, and waste.

Detailed AI logs help chefs and students make decisions based on real evidence that directly affects results. But when central offices control the data, these tools can turn into shallow metrics, hiding real differences in performance and taking control away from the people who actually cook. My main concern is simple, data should help us see and improve our teaching, not just protect a story. If we lose access to the details, we lose the chance to really get better and help our students, and the kitchen loses its voice.

Pipefitting

I am Paul, and I teach pipefitting here. Over time, I've noticed many opinions about what makes good training. I tend to keep to myself on campus. Some people think I work too slowly or avoid big projects. My colleague Will is the college's go-to example. He builds long overhead mains and complex rack systems that look impressive in photos. Students say his classes move quickly and feel like real job sites, and administrators often mention those reviews in meetings.

When the college introduced artificial intelligence into layout and installation from day one, I was actually pleased at first. Students began using smart levels and laser measuring tools that automatically recorded distances, slopes, support spacing, clearances, and tie-in points. The system could check if a two-inch drain had the right quarter-inch-per-foot slope. As fittings and valves were installed, they were scanned and added to a live 3D model of each system.

The platform checked each run against the isometric drawing, manufacturer specs, and code. It flagged problems such as flat or back-pitched slopes, supports too far apart, misaligned flanges, incorrect gasket materials, and clashes with steel, ductwork, or cable trays. Every issue was time-stamped and linked to the student, instructor, project, and even the exact step, such as a branch tie-in on level two in week four. For me, wanting systems to pass inspection and last, it felt like finally having reliable eyes on every joint and hanger. In the first semester, the reports started to challenge the college's view of which sections performed best. In Section A, Will's section, the projects were big and dramatic. Students built long mains overhead, complex rack systems, and worked at what they called a real jobsite pace. Evaluations praised the class for its speed and hands-on approach. Photos of Will's projects appeared in recruitment slides and on the college website.

But the artificial intelligence logs told a different story. On a typical project, 35 to 40 per cent of runs needed slope corrections. Three or four spools per line had to be cut again. Pressure tests failed about 30 per cent of the time because of leaks at flanges or threaded joints. Clash reports showed repeated conflicts with structural members and electrical conduits that needed rework after a walkthrough.

Section B looked different on the surface smaller, rarely photographed projects, and some student complaints about pace. Yet the data showed that under 10% of runs needed slope adjustment, over 95% of supports were in spec, and clashes were rare. First-pass pressure test success was 90%. For the first time, the college saw in concrete numbers which students produced piping that passed inspection and required less rework.

As more data came in and section comparisons became clearer, I saw people start to talk about the results differently. At first, instructors could see detailed slope maps, hanger layouts, clash reports, and test histories for every project. I used these records in debriefs to show students where a branch's slope was off or how adding a hanger stopped sagging. Will could have done the same, but the numbers made some people uncomfortable. They did not fit the college's idea of excellence. Soon, access to detailed logs was reduced. Instructors got simplified section scores and color coded blocks instead of full project histories. The more detailed dashboards went mostly to research and assessment committees, who turned them into safe, general statements like overall code compliance above 94% and fewer rework hours across the program. During my annual review, the dean showed one of these new dashboards, quickly scrolled past a page with slope and support data by section, and stopped on a slide with summary bars.

The dean said, "we are very pleased that the program overall is meeting our quality benchmarks. At the same time, we are concerned that the average project size in your section is below the program target. Going forward, we would like you to take on larger builds and increase the sense of real jobsite pace, while keeping your quality metrics in line with the department average." No one discussed first-pass pressure-test rates, slope corrections, or clashes avoided. There was no mention that my students had far fewer leaks and code issues than the flagship section featured in most college photos.

For instructors like me and for apprentices doing the hands-on work, the same data means something else. The raw artificial intelligence logs are the best teaching tool I've had. I can pause a model and show a student exactly where a drain line started to flatten or where a missing hanger could cause sagging. I can review each step from layout to final test and connect careful work to a clean first-pass pressure test. I've used these records to back up my fundamentals-based approach, showing that smaller builds and a slower pace lead to less rework and fewer failures, and that rushing schedules quickly leads to slope problems, clashes, and leaks.

From my vantage point, the bureaucracy dislikes this pipefitting scenario because it cuts directly across. From where I stand, the bureaucracy doesn't like this pipefitting scenario because it challenges its control. The artificial intelligence system removes uncertainty and changes the story. It shows, with clear data, that Will's high-profile section has more slope errors, clashes, and failed pressure tests than my basics-focused section, which the college has mostly ignored. It reveals the gap between titles and real skill, highlighting the results of a low-status instructor over a heavily promoted program used in recruitment and budget talks. Real-time dashboards make accountability immediate. A slope violation or failed test one day is visible the next, leaving less room for slow committees and vague talk about improvement. Ours and recurring code issues also shift the balance of leverage. We can point to patterns and show that a tight schedule is causing rework, or that a certain layout will definitely clash with other trades in a shared space. These claims are backed by data from the system itself.

In the end, the core issue is whether data will empower improvement or be used to defend old stories. If faculty lead, clear metrics can drive lasting quality. If decision-makers filter uncomfortable results, real lessons get hidden. The only path to real program excellence is to confront and act on what the data truly shows.

Truck Driving

I'm Max, and I direct the Commercial Truck Driving program at this college. Over the years, I've watched technology reshape our field. On campus, I'm recognised for insisting on strict safety standards: full pre-trip inspections and safe following distances. My colleague Ed, meanwhile, is known as the program’s star.

When the college put artificial intelligence into every lesson, I actually liked it at first. Each training truck received a telematics unit that logged speed, braking force, gear changes, lane position, following distance, and fuel use, along with a digital pre-trip checklist that recorded which items were actually inspected and how long the inspection took. Dashcams and side cameras began tagging hard brakes above a set G-force threshold, lane departures, following distances under 2 seconds, missed turn signals, and near-miss collisions. Every event was time-stamped and tied to a specific student, instructor, route segment (such as city loop, mountain grade, or night freeway), and even to weather conditions. For the first time, the program could see not just who finished the route, but also who maintained safe following distances on wet downhill stretches, who actually touched each pre-trip point, and who drove like a safe, employable professional.

By the middle of the term, the data showed a sharp contrast between sections. In Section A, Ed's section, the story still looked very good on the surface. Students described the class as fun and less stressful. Route times were fast, and employers saw photos of smiling students and shiny trucks in college materials. However, the artificial intelligence logs showed a different pattern. In Ed's section, about forty per cent of highway miles were driven more than five miles per hour over the limit. Hard-brake events averaged 6 per 10 driving hours. The following distance dropped under two seconds in roughly one-third of samples. More than a quarter of students skipped at least one critical brake or coupling check on the pre-trip.

In my Section B, my focus on accountability and best practices led to a different outcome. Students sometimes shared concerns that my expectations—slower driving, strict adherence to mirror checks, and thorough pre-trips—were demanding. My satisfaction scores were lower, and route times were slower. Yet the performance data confirmed the impact of disciplined leadership: speeding events in Section B were rare, hard-brake events averaged just 1 per 10 hours, and following distance remained above 3 seconds in over 90% of samples. Critical pre-trip checks were completed more than 95% of the time. Under my leadership, students also achieved between 0.5 and 0.8 miles per gallon higher through smoother shifting and steady driving. Throughout, a single chart could now illustrate clear, measurable advantages—lane departures were 3 per 100 miles versus 14, and missed critical pre-trip items were 4% in Section B, versus 27% in Section A. These results underscored the challenge of maintaining the claim that both sections were equally excellent.

Initially, instructors had access to comprehensive logs, which I used to deliver high-impact feedback sessions. I paused video clips at critical moments—when a student let the following distance shrink on a wet downhill grade or when a student skimmed past brake chamber checks in a rushed pre-trip. I used these timelines to demonstrate precisely how early gear changes on a hill could safeguard the engine and avert hard braking. This data validated the approach I have advocated for years; it provided evidence that prioritising safety standards produces measurable, superior outcomes.

Then meetings changed. Comparisons grew uncomfortable. Ed stayed the program's public face, but data revealed his section was riskier. Leadership tightened AI controls—access was cut, leaving only scores and colour codes. The new message: AI measured safety above 92 per cent, route efficiency up by 8 per cent. I thought, "What?"

In my annual review, I sat across from the dean while one of these new dashboards filled the screen. The dean quickly clicked past a page showing speeding, hard-brake events, and following distance by section, then stopped on a slide of summary bars. The dean said, "We are very pleased that the program overall is meeting our safety benchmarks. At the same time, we are concerned that your average route time is significantly above the program target and that student satisfaction in your section is below the department average. Going forward, we would like you to move closer to the program norms on pace and student experience while keeping these safety indicators in an acceptable range." There was no discussion of the fact that my students almost never missed critical pre-trip items, that their following distances were safer, or that they had fewer hard brake events and better fuel efficiency than the star section.

For instructors like me, and for students at the wheel through rain and darkness, this data is transformative. The raw AI logs have become my most effective teaching tool. I guide students step by step through mountain descents, showing how anticipatory actions like early downshifting prevent runaways. I replay near-misses, highlighting the precise moment a following distance collapses and a hard brake becomes unavoidable. Demonstrating the value of complete pre-trip checks, I present concrete evidence that thoroughness dramatically reduces risk. Armed with this information, I strongly advocate for my rigorous approach: whenever schedules are compressed or we attempt to match Ed's real-world pace, negative safety consequences follow. The data empowers effective, leadership-driven change.

In my view, this scenario challenges the traditional approach to institutional leadership. The AI system eliminates ambiguity, providing clear evidence of instructor effectiveness, the risks in current practices, and the veracity of success narratives. Hard data now shows that my section outperforms the star section on concrete safety measures. This creates a new paradigm: one in which visible leadership aligns with demonstrated competence, and in which accountability is immediate and direct. Yesterday's speeding or missed pre-trip checks are instantly visible; there is little space for delay or ambiguity. Leadership now means driving real performance, not just maintaining appearances.

Because the logs provide clear evidence to instructors and students, they shift the balance of power. Now we can show, with data, if a schedule encourages unsafe speeds or a route plan limits full pre-trip checks; such claims are harder to ignore. Whether this technology improves the program or becomes just another control depends on who decides what gets measured, how scores are used, and how results are reported. If faculty and apprentices influence these decisions, the system can help train safer drivers. But if central offices hold control, the bureaucracy may resist or dilute the system, turning detailed records into oversimplified scores that protect its version of program quality.

Medical Assisting

My name is Lydia, and I teach in the Medical Assisting program at this college. I have been here long enough to see more than one new system arrive, promising to modernise the clinic. On campus, I have a particular reputation. I am the instructor students describe as too serious, and my colleague Angel is the one praised. Angel runs the fast, smooth classes that externship sites and administrators like to highlight.

When the college wired artificial intelligence into every lab and simulated clinic day, I actually liked it at first. Students began to room standardised patients with tablets linked to the electronic health record. Every tap and scan was recorded. The system captured whether they used two identifiers, such as name and date of birth, whether they clicked through the hand hygiene checklist, which history of present illness and review of systems questions they selected, and how they documented chief complaints, allergies, and past history.

Smart vital sign carts recorded blood pressure, pulse, temperature, oxygen saturation, and respiration. They also recorded whether the cuff size was appropriate, how long the student waited before repeating an abnormal reading, and whether values were entered in the correct fields. For injections, the system logged the site choice, needle size, entry of the lot number and expiration date, and whether the three checks and six rights were completed on-screen. During electrocardiogram labs, sensors confirmed lead placement order and contact quality. During phlebotomy, scanners tracked the tube order of draw and label accuracy. Every action was stamped and tagged with student identification, instructor, section, and a specific scenario, a type two diabetes follow-up in week five. For someone like me, who cares deeply about safe medication practice and clean documentation, it felt like finally having a clear record of what actually happened in the room.

By week eight, the dashboards showed a sharp contrast between two sections that the college had long described in very different ways. In Section A, Angel's section, clinics ran quickly. Students passed skills checkoffs on schedule. Standardized patients reported feeling well cared for. Course evaluations praised confidence and real clinic speed. On the surface, it looked like the model other instructors were supposed to follow. However, the artificial intelligence logs told another story. In Angel's section, roughly thirty-eight per cent of encounters were missing a second identifier. Hand hygiene was skipped or timed inaccurately in about 1 in 4 roomings. Nearly 30% of diagnostic codes were either nonspecific or did not match the documented reason for the visit.

Injections were marked complete even when the system flagged missing numbers. Medication lists were often left unreconciled when a refill or an over-the-counter supplement was built into the scenario.

In my section, Section B, the pattern was almost the opposite. Students moved more slowly and complained that there were too many little details. My evaluations mentioned that I watched everything and that I made students restart if they missed a step. Yet the artificial intelligence data showed more than 95 per cent of encounters with two identifiers scanned, hand hygiene compliance around 98 per cent, fully correct medication reconciliation in 9 out of 10 visits, and coding errors that were rare and usually off only in specificity. By midterm, the near-miss medication error rate in my section was roughly one-third that in Angel's section. The documentation in my section more closely matched the clinic policy templates in both structure and content.

When these numbers were reported, I could sense that bureaucracy felt threatened. For years, the program had been sold upward on pass rates, externship placement, and glowing feedback that leaned heavily on smooth sections such as the Angel section. Now a single chart could show, for example, that Section A had twenty-seven near-miss medication errors for every one hundred encounters, while Section B had eight for everyone hundred, or that identity verification compliance in Section A was sixty-two per cent, while Section B was ninety-six per cent. Those numbers did not simply suggest improvement. They directly contradicted the institution's favorite story about who ran a strong section.

In response, leadership pulled raw access to artificial intelligence up to a small assessment group. Instructors were no longer given full logs that showed exactly where a pre-visit screen skipped allergy review or where a student documented a refill without reconciling the medication list. Instead, we received generic summaries. Each section was assigned one composite clinical safety score and one documentation quality score, with simple colour coding. At the same time, top-down targets appeared. All sections were told that they must reach a safety score of ninety by next term. In my annual review, I sat across from the dean while the new data filled the screen.

The dean scrolled past a page that briefly showed identity verification, hand hygiene, and near-miss error rates by section, then stopped on a slide with two large composite scores. The dean said, "we are pleased that your Safety Score is currently above the program average. However, your time per encounter is higher, and your student satisfaction is lower than we would like. Going forward, we expect you to maintain or improve this safety score while bringing your encounter times and student experience measures closer to the department averages." When I pointed out that my students were being penalized for taking a few extra seconds to recheck allergies and verify medications, the answer was simple. “The data is objective. Our job is not to argue with it but to respond to it.”

For instructors like me, and for students who are actually in the exam room with a standardized patient, the same data feels completely different. The artificial intelligence logs are the most powerful teaching tool I have ever used. I can replay an encounter and show a student the moment they skipped a second identifier or clicked past hand hygiene. I can pull up two versions of the same scenario and compare a sloppy medication reconciliation, full of omissions, with a careful one that catches supplements and recent changes. I have used this evidence to defend my detailed approach, showing that when we reduce station times or ask students to move faster, near misses and documentation errors rise almost immediately.

Bureaucracy does not dislike this Medical Assisting scenario because it opposes technology it dislikes artificial intelligence because it reveals the gap between titles and competence, between glossy narratives and real clinical safety, and between slow, committee-driven accountability and the immediacy of hard data. It shifts credibility and leverage toward practitioners and students and shortens the time leaders can hide behind the process. It becomes much harder to define quality around relationships, branding, and internal politics when the system shows, encounter by encounter, what actually happens in the exam room. Whether this technology becomes a tool for genuine learning or simply another layer of control depends on who controls the dashboard and who is allowed to speak for what the artificial intelligence system sees.

English Language Acquisitions

I teach in the English Language Acquisition program, and I have seen several different platforms come and go over the years. My name is Erin, the instructor some students and colleagues say is too focused on practice. My colleague Mary is the one the college likes to highlight. She teaches a morning class that is featured on campus tours. Student surveys praise her for her warmth and community-building, and her classes are known for their supportive energy.

When the college made every class use the same adaptive platform, I actually liked it at first. Students logged in on college Chromebooks and did daily tasks. They completed timed readings with questions, dictation exercises, short voice recordings, and wrote responses to prompts about work and community life. The system tracked reading levels, counted how many new word families students used correctly, measured listening accuracy on short dialogues, and recorded how often each student spoke into the microphone. It also tracked classroom patterns, like the balance between teacher and student talk, how many turns each learner took in pair work, and how much feedback focused on meaning instead of just accuracy. Every data point was labeled with section, instructor, and week of the term. For someone like me, who cares more about real language growth than just a positive classroom atmosphere, it finally felt like I had a clear record of what was happening.

By the middle of the semester, the dashboards began to contradict the college's comfortable narratives. The class had almost perfect attendance and almost no withdrawals. However, the artificial intelligence reports showed that most students had gained less than half a reading level. Many learners stayed at an average level. The system showed that a significant number of students went for entire weeks without recording more than 5 speaking turns.

In my evening section, things look different. I assign regular homework and encourage students to speak, even when they're shy or tired after work. I got a lot of complaints about too many corrections and too much work. My section had some early withdrawals, and no one would call it an easy class. But the data showed something else: students who started using conditionals in speaking doubled their active vocabulary. The artificial intelligence logs showed each student averaged 40 to 60 recorded speaking turns per week and clearly improved their intelligibility scores.

The platform made these differences easy to see. One chart showed that in Mary's class, teacher talk made up about 70% of class time, and students spoke an average of 30 words per class. In my evening class, teacher talk was about 40%, and students averaged around 180 words per class. Another report showed that students from my section were passing independent placement tests into higher levels, while many from the popular morning section repeated the same level, even with A grades and positive comments. For the first time, the college could see, week by week, where language development slowed down or sped up, broken down by instructor, schedule, and teaching style instead of just level numbers.

For years, the program was judged by headcount, retention, student satisfaction, and a few success stories about students getting jobs or moving on to college-level classes. Those measures favored Mary's morning community-building section and made my evening class look like a problem. The artificial intelligence data changed that story. It showed that real gains in reading, listening, and speaking were happening in the very section leadership had quietly thought about cutting.

In response, leadership started to limit who could see the data. Instructors lost access to detailed reports for each activity and student. Instead of seeing exactly how many speaking turns a learner took or how their listening accuracy changed from week four to week eight, we only got simplified growth scores and color-coded section averages. Institutional research turned the data into safe claims like overall English language proficiency gains of 0.8 levels per term. At the same time, new top-down targets appeared for average-level gains, without real input from teachers who knew that helping some students grow by 0.5 levels with strong foundations might be better than pushing everyone to chase a full-level jump.

During my annual review, the dean brought up new data, quickly skipped past a page showing teacher talk time and student speaking turns by section, and stopped on a slide with two composite scores. The dean said, "we are pleased that your students show strong growth, but we are concerned about your higher withdrawal rate and lower satisfaction scores. Going forward, we want you to maintain these growth numbers while improving retention and student experience to match the flagship sections." When I pointed out that my students spoke much more in class and that many were moving up to higher levels and entering the workforce, the answer was simple: the data is objective. The artificial intelligence system shows that classes with high retention show almost no change in speaking confidence, while a less popular section produces learners who can navigate job interviews, talk with teachers at their children's schools, and handle real conversations in the community. It exposes exactly what bureaucracy prefers to blur. It reveals the gap between popularity and effectiveness, between feel-good stories and measurable language growth, and between the people who are supposed to hold leadership positions and the people who actually help adults learn English. Whether this technology becomes a tool for real learning or simply another way to protect existing stories depends on who controls the dashboard and who is allowed to speak for what the system shows.

GED Program

My name is Jacinda, and I teach GED preparation at a career and technical college. I teach reading, math, social studies, and science in day and night classes, but only reading and math are leveled. Social studies and science are not. On paper, the pathway looks straightforward, yet my classes are always mixed in ability. In the same term I might teach a grade 2 reader alongside a grade 7 reader, a student strong in basic math but weak in basic reading, and a student who writes well in Spanish but not yet in English.

For students who progress smoothly, the sequence is predictable. They usually spend one term in Reading Level 1 and one term in Math Level 1, then complete Math Levels 2 and 3 in one term each. After finishing reading and math, they typically take one term of social studies and one term of science. The hybrid format complicates this, because the platform data shows that students who come to campus for higher-level work tend to be more independent and engaged, while many who stay online remain at lower levels longer or leave.

When the college adopted adaptive AI platforms, I used everything available. The systems start with a skills check, build personalized study plans, provide step-by-step tutoring, and support writing and accessibility needs. They also track growth, time on task, rereads of directions, and revision behavior, tagging activity by student, subject, time of day, and week. That data gives me a clearer map of what is happening and helps me group students and guide instruction based on evidence.

This is where the Bureaucratic Black Box shows up. The program is easy to defend when it looks neat from the outside, with clean levels and predictable pacing. AI disrupts that narrative by making learning patterns visible across levels, subjects, and delivery formats. AI shifts the focus from "what is wrong with the student" to "what is happening in the system," and once those patterns are measurable, the institution either has to redesign around the real learning map or try to push the evidence back into the dark.

Chapter 6

The Problem Was Never the Student

Education System Failure

Students in Career and Technical Education often face challenges unrelated to motivation or talent. Instead, they run into barriers that are not always visible in the classroom or lab. These can include dyslexia when reading medication guides or prep lists. Other examples include attention-deficit/hyperactivity disorder during long diagnostic procedures, low vision during weld inspections or food safety checks, hearing loss in shop environments, and mobility issues on ladders and scaffolds. Trauma and anxiety during tests and autism during service or patient interactions are also common. In the past, instructors might have labeled these students as not ready, inconsistent, too slow, or not a good fit. They noticed missed steps, incomplete work, or withdrawal, but often missed the underlying reasons.

AI systems in these programs take a different approach. Students use scan tools, weld cameras, kitchen stations, trucks, layout apps, listening platforms, and GED tutors. These tools record their work as it happens, not just the final outcome. This helps instructors see how a student made a mistake or achieved success. It also shows which steps were skipped, which part of the text was confusing, where a tremor affected welding, when noise made instructions hard to hear, and how anxiety affected test timing.

ADHD & Executive Function – Automotive Service

In the Automotive Service program, Caleb has Attention Deficit Hyperactivity Disorder and struggles most with the invisible parts of the job, tracking multi-step diagnostic routines, remembering where he left off, and organizing his time in the lab. He understands engines, but under pressure, he skips steps, forgets tests, and loses tools.

The college's AI diagnostic system becomes more than a grading tool for him. As Caleb connects the scan tool and opens a repair order, the AI overlays a personalized checklist on his tablet to verify concern, check fluid levels, scan for codes, inspect connectors, run live data tests, confirm root cause, and then authorize parts. It highlights the current step and dims the others, only revealing the next step when he completes the current one.

When he gets distracted, wandering off to help another student or jumping ahead to a part replacement, the system notices idle time or out-of-sequence actions and gently prompts him: "You've skipped the charging system test, run that next?" It also tracks how long jobs actually take him and suggests realistic time blocks, breaking large projects into smaller segments that fit his attention span.

Over the semester, Caleb does not suddenly become organized in the traditional sense, but his completion rate on full diagnostic flows increases, his forgotten-step errors drop sharply, and he starts to trust that he can handle complex jobs when the process is scaffolded. For him, AI is not just a performance monitor; it is a support that quietly fills the executive function gaps that used to hold him back.

Dyslexia – Practical Nursing

In the Practical Nursing program, Amina has dyslexia. She learns quickly in hands-on labs and verbal explanations, but dense medication guides, care plans, and charting templates overwhelm her. She worries about falling behind on pharmacology and documentation standards. The college's AI reading assistant is integrated directly into the EHR training platform. When Amina opens a medication monograph, she can tap an icon to have the AI read aloud at the speed she controls. The system highlights each line as it is spoken and allows her to click on a term like contraindication or titration for a simplified explanation in plain language, with an option for a short video or visual.

During documentation practice, the AI can transform blocks of text into structured outlines: Assessment → Intervention → Response → Follow-up, so she can see the shape of what she is reading. When she writes nurses notes, an AI tool checks not just spelling but clarity and structure, flagging missing elements rather than punishing her for letter reversals or slow typing.

Amina still works harder than some classmates to get through reading, but she is no longer locked out by the format. She can engage with the same clinical information as everyone else, at a pace and in a modality that works for her, and the program can assess her nursing judgment rather than her reading speed alone.

Hearing Loss – Commercial Truck Driving

Luis is in the Commercial Truck Driving program and has hearing loss in one ear. In a regular yard setup, engines are running and other students are practicing, so he has trouble hearing instructions and worries about missing warnings.

The AI telematics and coaching system adds visual support. Before each maneuver, his tablet shows a simple sequence of diagrams for the pull up, wheel turn, cone placement, and mirror reference points. As he drives, an AI display on the dash gives non audio cues. The wheel or seat vibrates when he gets close to a cone, an icon changes when his angle is off, and a signal tells him to stop and check around the truck.

Instructor instructions also go through a caption app linked to their headset, so when someone says "Stop there, straighten the wheels, and check your trailer," the words appear on a screen near the dash. The AI does not make the yard quiet. It makes sure key information reaches Luis in a form he can use. When he takes his CDL test, he is judged on backing, lane control, and safety, not on how well he hears shouted directions.

Low Vision – Welding

In the Welding program, Sofia has low vision. She can see large shapes and high-contrast images but struggles to read small print on equipment dials, interpret fine details in weld beads, or see subtle defects by eye. The AI weld vision system, originally adopted to score bead quality, becomes her second pair of eyes. When she finishes a pass, she positions the camera over the bead, and the system immediately magnifies and enhances the image on a high contrast tablet display. It outlines the bead in bold color, zooms in on suspect sections, and labels potential issues: undercut, porosity, and inconsistent travel speed.

The system can also read key features aloud average bead width acceptable. Porosity low. Undercut moderate on the right third recommends slower travel at the end. Instead of relying solely on visual inspection, Sofia can see her welds through AI analysis plus audio feedback. In addition, the helmet HUD shows amperage and voltage in large, high contrast digits rather than tiny, hard to dial on the machine. She still has to master hand skills and technique like any other welder, but AI shifts the evaluation from "Can you see this tiny defect?" to "Can you respond to feedback and improve your work?"

Autism & Social Communication – Medical Assisting

Noah is in the Medical Assisting program and is on the autism spectrum. He does well with procedures and paperwork, but patient conversations make him tired and confused. He worries about saying the wrong thing or missing tone and body language cues. The simulation AI tracks more than technical steps. After practice visits, it breaks down his interaction, showing how many open questions he asked, whether he used reflective statements, how often he interrupted, and when the patient seemed confused. Key takeaway: For Noah, tailored AI feedback translates social communication into learnable actions, making conversations less daunting. Clear, specific feedback helps Noah translate patient care into manageable actions. This allows him to build social communication routines with confidence.

Mobility Impairment – Carpentry

DeShawn is in the Carpentry program and has limited mobility in one leg after an accident. He can stand and move, but climbing ladders, kneeling for long periods, and carrying heavy materials tire him quickly. He worries that others think he cannot do the work. The AI layout and measurement system helps him. With laser measurers and a layout app, he marks and checks measurements from a steady spot. Instead of climbing to check alignment, he uses a mounted tablet that shows an overlay of the planned wall on the studs and flags any misalignment.

Instructors assign him layout, verification, and cut planning tasks, while classmates handle more ladder work. The AI notes that his layouts are accurate and require fewer corrections than average. His grade is based on decision quality and precision, rather than physical output. This approach ensures the program values technical planning, not just physical carpentry tasks.

Language & Hearing – English Language Acquisition (ELA)

Linh is in the English Language Acquisition program. She is learning English and is hard of hearing. Fast speech in a noisy classroom is hard for her to follow. Traditional listening exercises with short audio clips played once or twice leave her frustrated and behind. An AI captioning and practice system changes this. During class, the instructor's words appear as real-time captions on Linh's tablet, with key vocabulary highlighted. After class, the AI creates short video clips with matching captions that she can slow down, replay line by line, or switch to simpler wording. The system tracks which sounds she confuses and gives her practice on those patterns. In summary, AI support ensures Linh's success is measured by her real language growth and full class participation, not by limitations in hearing or processing speed.

Dyslexia in Level 1 Reading and Math

Maya enrolls in Level 1 Reading and Math GED classes after years of avoiding school because reading is hard for her. She has undiagnosed dyslexia. Letters move, directions blur, and by the end of a paragraph, she cannot remember the start. In a regular class, she would sit in the back and stay stuck. On the AI GED platform, each reading and math task has options she can change. She can switch to a dyslexia-friendly font, increase line spacing, and press a button to hear each word as it's highlighted. When she taps a word like 'approximate' or 'proportion,' the system provides a brief definition and an illustration.

In math, she notices she mostly misses problems with long word prompts, even when she knows how to do the calculation. For example, the AI starts giving her shorter versions first, then the full GED-style problem. It can read the problem aloud, break it into numbered steps, and give her space to mark key words. Her progress screen shows more than right or wrong. It shows that she understands well when text is read aloud and broken into parts, and that she chooses good strategies when the format does not get in the way. Her instructor can see that the issue is access, not effort. With the AI handling text layout and support, Maya can focus on thinking.

Her reading level begins to rise, and she starts to believe she can move to Level 2.

Attention Deficit Hyperactivity Disorder, Executive Function - GED

Andre attends an evening level 2 class after work. He has ADHD and struggles more with time and focus than with content. Without support, he starts well but loses track during long assignments, forgets which skills he was practicing, and leaves work unfinished. Instructors have called him inconsistent and unreliable. On the AI platform, he sees only three tasks at a time, such as a reading passage, a few math problems, and a short writing prompt. A progress bar shows these three. When he finishes them, the bar fills, and the next set appears. If he gets stuck on a problem and clicks away, the system notices and offers a hint or an easier warm-up. A tailored AI structure allows Andre's academic strengths to be visible, ensuring fairness in assessment and focus on what he truly knows.

Anxiety and Trauma in GED

Rosa is in a level 3 math and reading class on the weekend, getting ready for the GED next term. She has a history of trauma and strong test anxiety. When stressed, she freezes, her mind goes blank, and one bad quiz makes her feel she does not belong in school. Timed practice tests in the old system would likely have pushed her out. The system in level 3 works differently. On a practice GED reading test, it tracks her score and timing on each question. It notices she spends a lot of time on the first questions in a passage and then rushes through the rest.

The next time she logs in, it offers a warm-up mode with one passage, more time, and quick feedback before a full time set. After each practice, the AI creates a report that separates skills she has not learned from skills that break down under time pressure. Rosa and her instructor can see she often answers some question types correctly when there is no time limit but misses them when the clock is tight. The problem is not that she cannot read at the GED level, but that anxiety affects her timing and choices.

With this information, her instructor creates short practice sessions to make the format more familiar. The AI gradually reduces the time as Rosa's confidence increases. When Rosa takes the official exam, she knows from the data that she has already answered GED-level questions correctly many times. AI transforms test prep from confusing failures to a clear picture of what she knows and how stress affects her. Exia and Recipe-Heavy Prep. Finally, in Culinary Arts, Layla enrolls because she likes cooking at home, but printed recipes and long prep lists have always been hard for her.

In this program, an AI kitchen assistant runs on every station tablet. When Layla logs in, the system loads the day's recipes and converts them to a dyslexia-friendly font with more spacing. She can press a button to hear each step while the words are highlighted. Instructions appear as short, numbered steps with simple icons for tools and equipment. AI also tracks time. When Layla takes longer on knife prep, the system adjusts her schedule, so she is not always behind. If she pauses on a step, such as "deglaze with wine," she can tap it and see a short video of what to do.

Her instructors use a dashboard to distinguish her reading challenges from her cooking abilities. When she understands the steps, her knife skills and seasoning are strong. Instead of focusing on reading speed, AI highlights how she performs when directions are clear. She independently completes full recipes at her station, demonstrating her capability without copying others. The key takeaway is that reducing reading barriers reveals her true cooking skills.

Cerebral Palsy and Fine Motor Skills -On the Line

Marco has cerebral palsy that affects his fine motor control. He can move around the kitchen and use most tools, but tasks needing speed and precise cuts or garnish placement are harder for him. In a typical kitchen, he might be seen as too slow for the line. A vision system that grades knife skills and plating helps adjust tasks rather than just judging them. When Marco practices cuts, the system tracks average size and variation. It shows a large image on the station screen and marks where his dice are too big or too small. It also suggests changes like a different grip, a slower rhythm, or a different board position.

During service practice, the AI tracks speed and accuracy. Instructors can see his cuts start slower, but his consistency improves, and his waste is lower than many classmates. They adjust station roles so Marco often handles work where precision and yield matter more than speed, such as portioning proteins, checking temperatures, and finishing plates. Because the AI logs show strong portioning accuracy and safe temperatures, grading can reflect his skills rather than how quickly he can make many identical cuts. The system does not remove his disability. It makes his strengths and needs clear so the program can plan a path that fits him and the trade.

Low Vision and Food Safety

Nina has low vision and struggles to read small labels, see color changes, or notice cross-contamination risks on a busy line. She knows undercooked meat or spoiled food can harm people, but she cannot always see the visual cues that others use. In this program, an AI food safety system acts as a second set of eyes. Cameras at each station track cutting boards, raw and cooked items, and tools.

When Nina starts to prep poultry, the system highlights her cutting board on the screen and says “raw poultry board.” If it detects ready-to-eat food in the same area, it shows a warning and plays an audio alert. Smart thermometers and sensors announce temperatures aloud and display them in large numbers. When she checks the chicken, she hears "162 degrees… 165 degrees safe." In storage, when she scans an item, the AI says the product name, storage area, and use-by date.

Nina is graded on how she responds to this feedback, whether she fixes cross-contamination, reheats to a safe temperature, and labels correctly when the system gives information. AI lets the program judge her food safety decisions and habits, not just her eyesight.

Autism - Chaos of Service

Jonah is on the autism spectrum. He loves the predictable logic of recipes, but live service makes him anxious. The noise, shouted tickets, overlapping requests, and quick priority changes overwhelm him. In a regular kitchen, he might be pushed into back-of-house prep only, never getting a fair chance to learn line skills. Here, the AI ticket system acts as a social and sensory buffer. Instead of relying only on shouted orders, Jonah's station tablet displays tickets in a structured, color-coded list: items due soon, items in progress, and items waiting on other stations. Each ticket breaks into steps with simple icons: start protein, fire garnish, plate, and wipe, and a timeline that updates in real time as other stations mark their progress.

When the kitchen gets noisy, Jonah can lower the audible alerts and rely on visual cues and gentle haptic feedback on a wristband: a small vibration when it is time to fire the next component, and a different pattern when a rush of new tickets comes in. After service, the AI generates a timeline of his station: where he fell behind, where he waited too long, and where he hit the perfect timing. It lets him replay the rush as a clear sequence instead of a blur. Instructors can see that with structured visual information, Jonah's timing and quality are excellent. AI helps turn chaotic, unstructured pressure into a pattern he can read and respond to. Instead of being told vaguely to move faster, he gets precise, data-backed coaching on how to adjust his workflow. He earns line experience based on performance, not on his comfort with shouting and noise.

Low Vision - Bead Inspection

Eli has low vision. He can see shapes and movement, but small details like pinholes, undercut, and slight waviness are hard for him to spot, even with a magnifying glass. In a regular welding class, he would often hear "look closer, see that" and nod, even if he couldn't actually see what the instructor meant. His welds would be judged on things his eyes couldn't clearly make out. In this program, each lab booth has an AI weld vision system. After Eli finishes a bead, he puts the test plate into a scanner. The AI takes a picture and displays it on a screen at its station. It zooms in and traces the bead, marking likely defects such as porosity, undercuts, uneven width, and high crowns one by one.

His instructor can show comparisons, such as Eli's bead today versus last week, or his bead versus a sample that meets the standard. The AI measurements show his consistency is improving, even when he can't see it. Over time, Eli connects certain hand motions, speeds, and sounds with what the AI calls acceptable work. The program can grade him on weld quality and growth rather than on his ability to inspect like someone with full sight.

Tremor - Fine Control

Brianna has an essential tremor that appears when she holds something in front of her, which is required for welding. On some days, her hands shake, and her weave patterns and arc length change. In a lab, her welds might be marked down, and she might be moved toward another trade. The AI system on her welding machine records torch angle, travel speed, arc length, and current in real time. As she welds, the screen shows her path alongside a target pattern and provides feedback such as 'speed high,' ' arc length growing,' and 'angle drifting.' After each pass, it produces a trace of her motion and marks the spots where the tremor pushed her off line.

Her instructor and disability services use this data to test changes, such as new grips, heavier handles, and work positions that provide her with more support. The AI shows the effect of each change. With a different rest position, her arc length variation drops by forty percent, even though the tremor remains. When grading, the program can look at how close her beads are to the standard, how much she has reduced variation over time, and how often she produces welds that meet requirements.

Hearing Loss - Noisy Labs

Mateo has hearing loss and uses hearing aids. He also wears hearing protection in the lab, which makes speech even harder to hear. The welding shop is loud with grinders, fans, arc noise, and the sound of moving metal. Instructors often give quick verbal guidance from behind a hood or across booths. Mateo often misses corrections like “slow down” or “too far off,” and only later learns that his bead is off.

The program connects the AI weld monitoring system to a visual cue and caption setup. As he welds, the AI tracks his speed and arc position. When it sees an error, such as travel speed too fast, torch off-center, or arc length growing, it flashes an icon in the corner of its booth display. A turtle means slow down, a target means move back to center, and a short bar means move closer. The icons are large and placed where he can see them with a quick glance without lifting his hood.

In debriefs, the instructor's spoken comments are recorded and transcribed by AI, then lined up with the weld video. Mateo can replay a pass and read "Here I said pause, this is where your pool started to outrun you" at the moment it happened. Instead of holding on to bits of what he heard through noise and equipment, he gets a clear record of what was said and when. Over time, the AI pattern detection and visual feedback help him learn the needed adjustments even when he is not looking at the screen. He depends less on hearing live corrections and more on what he feels and sees in the puddle. His performance is no longer tied to how well he can hear in the lab.

Bureaucracy Hates How AI Can Help Students with Disabilities

AI support for disabled students challenges bureaucracy by showing that many student problems are actually design problems. When AI is built into real coursework, it reveals which changes help students succeed, for example text read aloud, chunking, captions, or different pacing. The story then shifts from the student is not ready to the environment that was not built for this student. The data can show that evening or online classes sometimes outperform main programs for disabled students. As AI makes exclusion visible and points to better options, it gives instructors and disability services more evidence and makes it harder for institutions to deny that many barriers came from their own choices.

PART III

Shared Patterns of Resistance: The Bureaucracy's Script

Chapter 7

AI and Change Agents

Is there a Difference? Or Are they the Same?

Artificial Intelligence (AI) and the human Change Agent seem to belong to different worlds. AI is a set of systems trained on data. The Change Agent is a person or group pushing institutions toward a more honest, merit-based future. One is written in code, the other in biography and conviction. Yet inside a technical college run by a Bureaucratic Black Box, they are treated much the same.

To bureaucracy, they share one unforgivable trait. Both insist that reality be measured rather than narrated. AI measures content quality, enrollment patterns, financial anomalies, and student performance in ways that are hard to spin. The Change Agent measures the same institution through classroom experience, policy analysis, and equity data. Both generate inconvenient truths that collide with official stories and threaten the unwritten agreement that protects administrative authority.

AI and the Change Agent act as translators of reality. AI turns institutional noise into signal, detecting patterns and making predictions about students, programs, and resources. The Change Agent turns human experience into diagnosis and argument, weaving together instructor stories, student confusion, contradictory policies, and gaps between rhetoric and reality into a case for reform. Where AI turns data into predictions, the Change Agent turns experience into evidence and critique. Both depend on access to information and pathways into decision-making, and both are dangerous to the Black Box because they reject curated versions of reality. They also share a commitment to merit over status. A specialized AI system does not care whether a student is popular or an instructor is favored. It checks whether the work meets the standard. The Change Agent asks similar questions. Does this policy improve learning or equity.

Does this process serve students or protect comfort. In a system built on symbolic authority, this focus on merit is intolerable. When AI shows that a celebrated program underperforms, it punctures the symbolic capital of those who built careers on that narrative. When the Change Agent points to data showing that "innovative" initiatives exist only on paper, they threaten leaders who rely on performative change.

Both also demand transparency in systems that rely on selective invisibility. AI needs visible data to score welds, flag financial irregularities, or forecast enrollment. The Change Agent seeks visibility into who approves what, how budgets move, which programs are underfunded, and where exclusion or retaliation appear. The Black Box survives on partial visibility just enough for reports and accreditation, not enough to challenge power. AI and the

Change Agent push for full visibility, from raw data behind the narrative to outcomes behind the branding. As a result, AI is framed as risky not only for ethical reasons but because it can reveal waste and failure. The Change Agent is labeled disruptive or not a good fit because they refuse to look away.

Their resistance follows the same pattern. AI projects are buried in ethics forms, pilots, and risk reviews that never scale. Change Agents are loaded with committees, tasks, and process hoops that sap their energy. AI becomes a compliance tool whenever it produces uncomfortable truths. The Change Agent becomes a culture problem whenever they name those truths. Both are contained. AI is limited to chatbots and low stakes tools that avoid budgets and staffing. Change Agents are kept off key committees, denied data, or shifted into safer roles. The goal is to cut both off from real power.

There is one key difference that makes their alliance so powerful. AI is a mirror. It reflects patterns in the institution but does not decide what they mean. In the hands of bureaucratic leaders, AI can be turned toward surveillance or justification as easily as accountability. The Change Agent is a voice. They interpret what the mirror shows and ask what it means when certain students have lower completion, when a praised program fails disabled students, or when burnout jumps after certain decisions. AI without the

Change Agent is mute and easily captured. The Change Agent without AI is easily dismissed as anecdotal.

Together, they create a threat the Black Box cannot easily absorb. AI supplies evidence that is hard to ignore. The Change Agent supplies analysis and moral argument that link this evidence to governance, policy, and resource allocation. AI confirms at scale what Change Agents have long seen in classrooms and meetings. Change Agents keep AI from becoming a neutral tool of control by insisting that its outputs be read through equity, student benefit, and merit-based accountability. This fusion data that contradicts institutional stories plus a human who refuses to bury that contradiction is what bureaucracy fears most.

This fear explains a recurring pattern. Leaders praise AI while sidelining those who might use it to demand reform, or they value Change Agents only as long as those people lack access to strong AI tools. AI is welcomed when it supports low stakes routines. Change Agents are welcomed when they stay in roles with no budget or policy authority. What is avoided is their combination in the same person or team, the welding instructor with AI quality data and assessment power, the nursing faculty member with simulation outcomes and a vote on resource allocation, the adult education leader connecting AI enrollment analysis to funding inequities. When data, narrative, and decisions come together, escape routes close.

AI will fail in education, not because the tools are weak, but because the system is designed to neutralize anything that reveals too much truth. Without empowered Change Agents, AI will be pushed into low impact roles or shut down once it exposes contradictions. Without AI, Change Agents will keep burning out, forced to argue with anecdotes and partial data. AI and the Change Agent are alike because they perform the same political function. They measure what institutions prefer to narrate, expose the gap between claims and reality, and lift merit over status. For that reason, both are treated as threats to a bureaucracy built on secrecy and symbolic authority. Any path to using AI in ways that truly serve students will depend on this uneasy partnership between the machine that reflects the truth and the human who refuses to let that truth be buried.

Chapter 8

Bureaucratic AI

When Technology Becomes an Extension of the Black Box

Weber's view of bureaucracy, as discussed by Newman, Mintrom, and O'Neill (2022), treats public administration as a machine run by rules and separated from elections and party politics. Officials are parts of this machine. Their authority comes from the office they hold, not from personal traits. Power rests in positions, jobs are filled on merit, and loyalty is to public service, not private interests. Job security, budget rules, and secrecy around operations protect offices from political pressure and keep administration rule based (Newman et al., 2022).

Newman et al., (2022) argue that this helps explain why digital technologies often strengthen bureaucracy. Computing, automation, and AI speed up information handling, add procedures, and raise the expertise needed to take part. In Weber's terms, they are upgrades to the machine. They extend administrative reach and make it harder for outsiders, including politicians, citizens, and frontline staff, to influence internal work. From this view, AI fits existing routines and supports the authority Weber described.

But Butt (2024) notes a tension. AI can support fairness, reduce bias, and improve due process only when systems are open, explainable, and subject to oversight. These needs clash with common bureaucratic practice. The same opacity and control over information that once protected administration now block the checks AI would need. The machine tends to adopt AI in ways that protect hierarchy, not invite challenge.

In technical colleges, this mix leads to what I call Bureaucratic AI. Leaders are wary of tools that give teachers and students clear performance data, such as welding cameras, medical simulators, or cybersecurity systems. These tools expose errors and uneven programs, which conflicts with the message that everything is fine. As Butt (2024) observes in government settings, keeping algorithms hidden becomes a way to avoid responsibility.

Discipline AI tools are labeled high risk or non-compliant, while tools such as writing assistants, chatbots, and AI enhancement platforms are adopted instead. These tools signal innovation but do not change who controls information. Data is filtered, access is limited, and insights are shaped to protect the story. This turns what Butt calls a danger to due process into a regular way of governing.

Bureaucratic AI also helps institutions look legitimate. In line with Butt's critique of performative compliance, colleges use AI as a branding tool. It becomes proof of innovation meant to impress accreditors, funders, and policymakers, while leaving unequal structures mostly in place. Administrators who manage institution wide AI systems are praised as forward thinking, while instructors who use real, discipline based AI tools are more likely to be seen as troublemakers or rule breakers. As a result, AI centralizes power instead of supporting Weber's idea of stable, rule bound roles, even while it is advertised as technological progress.

In the end, AI does not fall short because its algorithms are weak. It falls short because it is used inside systems that resist openness, shared power, and accountability. When these systems operate inside Weberian bureaucracies in education, AI becomes exactly what the structure permits: another layer of the Black Box. Unless the design of the institution itself is challenged and changed, AI in technical colleges will be neutralized in the same way these bureaucracies have long neutralized human change agents.

Chapter 9

Coexistence or Collision?

Whether AI, Change Agents, and Bureaucracy Can Live in the Same System

The question of whether Artificial Intelligence, Change Agents, and bureaucrats can coexist is not simply a question about technology. It is a question about power. AI is a force for transparency. Change Agents are forces for transformation. Bureaucracy is a force for preservation. These three forces do not merely interact within the institution; they collide, negotiate, and reshape one another. Their coexistence is possible, but only under conditions that fundamentally alter the architecture of decision-making.

At first glance, these forces seem compatible. AI can support administrative efficiency, reduce workload, and enhance compliance. Change Agents can translate innovation into measurable improvements and bridge leadership vision with classroom realities. Bureaucrats can provide structure, ensure safety, and maintain continuity during transitions. In theory, these roles form a balanced ecosystem in which technology drives improvement, leaders maintain order, and educators innovate. In practice, however, the institution is not a neutral ecosystem. It is a hierarchy designed to protect itself, and that design determines how these forces interact.

The Bureaucratic Black Box system functions as a closed loop. It rewards predictability, continuity, and procedural stability qualities that ensure bureaucracy's own survival. AI introduces unpredictability through data transparency. It reveals outcomes that bureaucratic leaders cannot fully script, curate, or control through narrative. Change Agents intensify this unpredictability by advocating for reforms that prioritize student outcomes over institutional comfort. Together, AI and Change Agents introduce visibility into a system that depends on opacity. They challenge the norms bureaucrats rely on to maintain authority. Under traditional conditions, coexistence is impossible because their missions conflict at the level of institutional identity.

Coexistence becomes possible only when specific transformations occur within the bureaucratic structure, beginning with bureaucracy relinquishing its monopoly on interpretation. In the current model, administrators control narratives, decision timelines, access to information, and claims to institutional legitimacy. AI disrupts this control by producing raw, unfiltered evidence. A welding analysis system that exposes grading inconsistencies or a student retention model that reveals inequitable outcomes shifts interpretive power away from administrators. For coexistence to occur, leaders must accept that they no longer own the truth and allow it to be interpreted collectively by faculty, students, and transparent AI systems.

The second requirement is a redefinition of authority. Bureaucracy traditionally views authority as positional, derived from title, office, and hierarchy. While Change Agents gain authority from performance, expertise, and results, and AI gains authority from data and accuracy These forms of authority can coexist only when institutions recognize that positional authority is not automatically superior. Hierarchies must be reshaped so expertise-driven and data-driven authority have real legitimacy. This means specialized instructors must have genuine decision-making power in AI adoption, and administrators cannot simply override evidence to preserve preferred narratives. Authority must become negotiated, shared, and validated by outcomes rather than status. Without this shift, coexistence remains impossible because traditional hierarchies cannot tolerate competing forms of legitimacy.

The third requirement is the removal of institutional secrecy. Bureaucracy thrives on selective visibility, unclear rules, opaque budgets, and decisions made out of sight, while AI and Change Agents require clarity and transparency. When secrecy is maintained, AI is reduced to a symbolic tool or blocked altogether. Institutions must commit to open data governance such as AI registries, bias audits, and transparent metrics to prevent bureaucrats from using ambiguity as a shield. With transparency enforced by policy, the bureaucracy shifts from a protective system to a collaborative one: AI provides evidence, Change Agents interpret it, and bureaucrats ensure implementation aligns with safety and compliance, allowing the three roles to function in alignment rather than opposition.

The fourth requirement is the protection of Change Agents. Bureaucratic culture often isolates, discredits, or excludes those who challenge accepted norms. Yet AI frequently confirms their observations by producing evidence of inefficiencies, inequities, or failures. When Change Agents are protected through policy, governance structures, and clear reporting lines, their work becomes institutional rather than personal. Bureaucrats become less likely to see them as threats and more likely to recognize them as contributors. AI then amplifies their capabilities instead of triggering retaliation. Once Change Agents are understood as structural actors instead of political risks, coexistence becomes far more realistic.

For coexistence to be productive, bureaucracy's core mission must shift from preserving the institution to protecting outcomes. When bureaucracy moves from protecting authority to stewardship, traditional roles harmonize, bureaucrats become facilitators of innovation, AI acts as a partner in oversight, and Change Agents become collaborators. In this reimagined system, bureaucrats provide structure, Change Agents offer vision, and AI supplies evidence and acceleration. This potent coexistence, however, is conditional. It requires dismantling the 'Black Box' through policies enforcing transparency, governance sharing authority, and a culture that prioritizes expertise over politics.

The truth is simple: AI, Change Agents, and bureaucrats can coexist, but not inside the system as it currently exists. Coexistence requires dismantling the mechanisms bureaucracy uses to protect itself and transform the institution at the level of its identity. Until that transformation occurs, the clash between these forces will remain predictable, inevitable, and destructive. The Black Box of institutional opacity mirrors the famous myth of Pandora's Box. The myth emphasizes that while the box's opening releases disruptive forces (the "evils"), the crucial outcome is the release of Hope. This duality is essential: the old system (the Black Box) must be forcefully broken open, a necessary, painful release to allow the powerful forces of AI and Change Agents to be fully unleashed. The Black Box cannot contain AI and Change Agents without neutralizing them. Only when it is forced open through policy, governance, and cultural awakening can these three forces finally work together to build the transparent, equitable, merit-driven institutions. Is there hope? Sure! Will it happen, that is the question.

Conclusion

By now, the Bureaucratic Black Box is no longer just a metaphor. It appears across welding booths, simulation labs, kitchens, trucks, clinics, pipe racks, language classrooms, and GED programs. This system protects authority and manages appearances through rules, relationships, and information control. Artificial Intelligence enters as both a mirror and a disturbance. Built into real work, it tracks weld beads, medication passes, brake checks, conduit runs, diagnostic routines, recipes, language use, and GED progress. It does not care who is popular. It records what happens. Often, it shows that quiet or overlooked sections produce safer, more skilled graduates than those highlighted in marketing.

Once this evidence exists, a shift occurs, and familiar metrics like enrollment, completion, and satisfaction are no longer sufficient. AI tools add what was missing. For example, how often are safety checks done? How much rework is required? Which sections pass inspection the first time? How many unnecessary parts are installed? How much do students actually speak? How far do disabled students progress when work is redesigned? Conflict starts when these findings collide with comfortable stories.

The response is to pull the detail upward and flatten it. Logs that instructors use for teaching move into leadership offices. Dashboards are reduced to composite scores and simple green indicators. Systems that reveal sharp differences are slowed, labeled as risky, or kept in endless pilots. Meanwhile, generic tools are shown off as proof of innovation. Instructors who use AI evidence to argue for better conditions or to question favored programs are treated as cultural problems. AI and human Change Agents both insist on measuring reality and centering outcomes over image. A self-protective bureaucracy treats that stance as a threat and moves to contain it.

Yet the same evidence can strengthen teaching. When instructors and students have direct access to detailed AI data, they use it to refine practice and standards. Welding teachers target specific errors. Nursing and medical assisting faculty use simulation logs to better prepare students. Instructors in heating and cooling, automotive, pipefitting, trucking, culinary arts, English language, and GED programs use performance records. These records show that careful, methodical teaching produces more proficient graduates.

For disabled students, these tools can shift the judgment from 'not ready' to 'capable'. AI supports reading, attention, perception, movement, communication, and testing. These supports allow real skill to appear. Difficulties once framed as a lack of effort or a poor fit start to look like design problems in courses, labs, and assessments. Many old beliefs about who belongs are exposed to environments that were never built with these learners in mind. AI drives the movement toward Inclusive Design and Universal Design for Learning (UDL). When the environment is the barrier, the environment must change.

AI, Change Agents, and bureaucracy are to coexist in ways that serve students. Decision-making must change. Transparency must be a normal practice. Data is collected to improve processes. It flows to the user who controls the process. This enables real-time adjustments. For example, a teacher can adjust a lesson based on live student performance metrics. A mechanic can check sensor data directly on the shop floor. Authority over what is measured and how it is read must be shared with those who know the discipline and live with the results. Change Agents must be protected when they present AI-based evidence of harm or inequity. Disabled students must be treated as central users whose needs shape ideas of good design.

These choices are not technical. They are matters of everyday governance. Leaders can share findings or keep them sealed. Chairs can back instructors whose results unsettle the story. Boards can treat openness and accessibility as real duties. The Black Box is strong, but it is a human design. Human designs can change. AI can be used to tighten control or to make the structure visible enough to challenge. What remains is to decide what kind of institution we are willing to maintain. We must decide how much truth we are prepared to act on.

References

- Amiri, S. M. H., & Islam, M. M. (2025).

  Enhancing Python programming education with an AI powered code helper: Design, implementation, and impact. *Software Engineering*, *11*(1), 1–17. https://doi.org/10.11648/j.se.20251101.11

- Botev, Z. I., Kroese, D. P., & Taimre, T. (2025).

  Data science and machine learning: Mathematical and statistical methods (2nd ed.). Chapman and Hall/CRC. https://doi.org/10.1201/9781003391173

- Brown, C., White, R., & Kelly, A. (2021).

  Teachers as educational change agents: What do we currently know? Findings from a systematic review. *Emerald Open Research*, *3*, 26. https://doi.org/10.35241/emeraldopenres.14385.1

- Butt, J. S. (2024). From bureaucracy to black box:

  Revolutionizing natural justice and due process in administrative law. *Acta Universitatis Danubius. Administratio*, *16*(1), 7–47.

- Cao, W., & Mai, N. (2025).

  Predictive analytics for student success: AI-driven early warning systems and intervention strategies for educational risk management. *Educational Research and Human Development*, *2*(2), 36–48.

- Ciubotaru, B. I. (2025).

  Generative AI and large language models: A comprehensive scientific review (Version 2). Preprints. https://doi.org/10.20944/preprints202504.0413.v2

- Dai, R., Thomas, M. K. E., & Rawolle, S. (2025).

  The roles of AI and educational leaders in:

  AI assisted administrative decision-making: A proposed framework for symbiotic collaboration. *Aust. Educ. Res.*, *52*, 1471–1487. https://doi.org/10.1007/s13384-024-00771-8

- Deshpande, T., & Sharma, K. (2025).

  Advancing artificial intelligence: An in-depth look at machine learning and deep learning architectures, methodologies, applications, and future trends. *International Journal of Intelligent Data and Machine Learning*, *2*(1), 8–13. https://doi.org/10.55640/ijidml-v02i01-02

- Ehrich, L. C., & English, F. W. (2024).

  Re-imagining leadership roles beyond the shadow of bureaucracy. *Education Sciences*, *14*(3), 331. https://doi.org/10.3390/educsci14030331

- Gerwing, C. (2016). Meaning of change agents within organizational change.

  Journal of Applied Leadership and Management, *4*, 21–40. http://www.journal-alm.org/article/view/17107

- Gokmenoglu, T., Dasci Sonmez, E., Durmus, C., & Karakullukcu, O. F. (2025).

  Empowering "resilience-building agents:" An analysis of physical education teachers' instructional intentions for disaster preparation. *International Journal of Disaster Risk Reduction, 111*, 105685. https://doi.org/10.1016/j.ijdrr.2025.105685

- Herodotou, C., Naydenova, G., Boroowa, A., Gilmour, A., & Rienties, B. (2020).

  How can predictive learning analytics and motivational interventions increase student retention and enhance administrative support in distance education? *Journal of Learning Analytics*, *7*(2), 72–83.

- Hu, A. (2024).

  Developing an AI-based psychometric system for assessing learning difficulties and adaptive system to overcome: A qualitative and conceptual framework. arXiv. https://arxiv.org/abs/2403.06284

- Humes, W. (2021).

  The "iron cage" of educational bureaucracy. *British Journal of Educational Studies*, *70*(2), 235–253. https://doi.org/10.1080/00071005.2021.1899129

- Jarrahi, M. H. (2018).

  Artificial intelligence and the future of work: Human-AI symbiosis in organizational decision making. *Business*

Horizons, *61*(4), 577–586.
https://doi.org/10.1016/j.bushor.2018.03.007

- Khine, M. S. (2024).

  Using AI for adaptive learning and adaptive assessment.

  In M. S. Khine (Ed.), *Artificial intelligence in education* (pp. 41–65). Springer Nature Singapore. https://doi.org/10.1007/978-981-97-9350-1_3

- Lumby, J. (2017).

  Distributed leadership and bureaucracy. *Educational Management Administration & Leadership*, *47*(1), 5–19. https://doi.org/10.1177/1741143217711190

- Mashhady, A., Khalili, H., & Sameti, A. (2022).

  Does change agent selection procedure matter? A strategic decision-making toward a more objective selection approach. *Leadership & Organization Development Journal*, *43*(8), 1157–1185. https://doi.org/10.1108/LODJ-01-2022-0041

- Newman, J., Mintrom, M., & O'Neill, D. (2022).

  Digital technologies, artificial intelligence, and bureaucratic transformation. *Futures, 136*. https://doi.org/10.1016/j.futures.2021.102886

- Nkadimeng, M. G., Murulane, K., & Telukdarie, A. (2024).

  Leveraging AI for unbiased analysis of emerging techniques in academic literature. In G. Natarajan, H. Zhang, & E. Ng (Eds.), *Proceedings of the 2024*

International Annual Conference and 45th Annual Meeting: Engineering Management Riding the Waves of Smart Systems, ASEM 2024 (pp. 79–88). American Society for Engineering Management.

- Phinla, W. (2023, November 4). *Innovative educators:*

  The change agent for driving the quality of education. SSRN. https://ssrn.com/abstract=5102799

- Praveena, T., & Anupama, K. (2025).

  Machine learning meets language learning: The transformative potential of artificial intelligence in English language instruction. *Human Research in Rehabilitation, 15*(1).

- Saini, J., Choudhary, S., & Walia, K. (2025).

  The future of AI in decision-making: Replacing or assisting humans? *International Journal of Sciences and Innovation Engineering, 2*(5), 751–778. https://doi.org/10.70849/IJSCI

- Sun, J. C., & Pratt, T. L. (2024).

  Navigating AI integration in career and technical education:

  Diffusion challenges, opportunities, and decisions. *Education Sciences, 14*(12), 1285. https://doi.org/10.3390/educsci14121285

- Ungvarsky, J. (2025). Change agent.

- In*Salem Press Encyclopedia*. von Eschenbach, W. J. (2021). Transparency and the black box problem: Why we do not trust AI. *Philosophy & Technology, 34*(4), 1607–1628. https://doi.org/10.1007/s13347-021-00477-0

- Wang, C. (2025).

  Behavioral computing for human factor security and safety in traffic and transportation. In *Human factor security and safety: A behavioral computing approach* (pp. 219–240). Springer Nature Singapore.

- Wang, X., Zhao, S., Xu, X., Zhang, H., & Lei, V. N. L. (2025).

  AI adoption in Chinese universities: Insights, challenges, and opportunities from academic leaders. *Acta Psychologica, 258*, 105160. https://doi.org/10.1016/j.actpsy.2025.105160

- Wang, Y. (2021).

  Artificial intelligence in educational leadership: A symbiotic role of human-artificial intelligence decision-making. *Journal of Educational Administration, 59*(6), 671–686. https://doi.org/10.1108/jea-10-2020-0216

- Weber, M. (1978). *Economy and society: An outline of interpretive sociology* (G. Roth & C. Wittich, Eds.). University of California Press

- Wireman, B. O. (1998, December 15).

  Characteristics of change agents. *Vital Speeches of the Day, 65*,152–154. https://www.proquest.com/magazines/characteristics change-agents/docview/221467520/se-2

About The Author

Dr. Jacinda Lay is a results-driven educational leader with deep experience in adult education, program management, curriculum development, and workforce-aligned learning. She currently teaches GED preparation, supporting learners across math, language arts, social studies, and science in day and evening settings. Her career includes faculty and instructional leadership roles spanning technical colleges, K–12 classrooms, and community-based organizations, including prior work as a director of education programs serving urban communities and families.

Dr. Lay is a State Advocate for Adult Education Fellow with the Coalition on Adult Basic Education and co-founded the Colorado Adult Education Coalition, where she helps guide strategy, governance, and stakeholder engagement. In September 2025, her advocacy work contributed to a gubernatorial proclamation recognizing Adult Basic Education and Family Literacy Week in Colorado. She is committed to building inclusive, innovative learning environments and advancing educator capacity through continuous improvement and professional development. Dr. Lay writes from lived proximity to institutional power. She knows what it is to stand on the outside and look in. Educational institutions present themselves as hierarchies governed by job titles, reporting structures, and written expectations that are blurred to seem real. Yet those embedded in career and technical education quickly learn that the formal hierarchy is often a façade. The real hierarchy operates behind the scenes, where authority is conferred not by position but by acceptance into an informal circle. She believes in meritocracy and equality, and that a person's worth should be measured by actions and contributions rather than political standing or organizational title.

That belief shapes how she works to create positive change. Her focus on student success, combined with leadership experience, helps her recognize when institutions become complacent. When opportunities appear, she acts with evidence and perspective. Those opportunities are rare, and she has learned not to expect them. She is accustomed to being told to "put a muzzle on it," to "stay in your lane," and to "keep moving along," yet she continues to advocate for truth, accountability, and better outcomes for learners.

www.ingramcontent.com/pod-product-compliance
Lightning Source LLC
LaVergne TN
LVHW050937210926
848482LV00013B/645
* 9 7 9 8 2 9 5 5 1 7 4 2 6 *